Quest for the
Mead of Poetry

MENSTRUAL SYMBOLISM IN
ICELANDIC FOLK AND FAIRY TALES

Hallfridur J. Ragnheidardottir

CHIRON PUBLICATIONS • ASHEVILLE, NORTH CAROLINA

www.ChironPublicatons.com
978-1-63051-369-6 paperback
978-1-63051-370-2 Hardcover
978-1-63051-371-9 ebook

Cover design and typesetting by Nelly Murariu
Printed in the United States of America.

Library of Congress Cataloging-in-Publication Data

To my son, Jón Ingi,
who has found his music.

And to his sons, Þorri and Halli.
May they, too, find theirs.

Acknowledgements

In the fall of 2004, a group of four trusted friends gathered in my home once a week for seven weeks and accompanied me through the seven tales in this collection. Within this protective circle, I was provided with an opportunity to test the ideas that had taken root in me. The project continued to evolve, and in 2006 I gathered a second group together.

In both instances our meetings were marked by sisterly ambiance, induced by the universal experience we shared with our ancestresses who spoke to us across the abyss of time in these tales. Looking back, this fruitful groundwork has itself taken on the aura of an enchanting tale.

My heartfelt thanks go to Arnfríður Hallvarðsdóttir, Sigríður Baldursdóttir, Sigurbjörg Einarsdóttir, my sister, Valgerður Jakobsdóttir, Áslaug Benediktsdóttir, Elísabet Þórðardóttir, Guðbjörg Stephensen, and Kolbrún Sæmundsdóttir.

I also extend my sincere thanks to Ami Ronnberg, curator of The Archive for Research in Archetypal Symbolism, who in 2003 entrusted me with writing an entry on Freyja intended for a book of symbols. It was at this point that the theme of menstruation pushed to the fore, much like the dissolving flow itself takes a young girl by surprise at her first bleeding. Delving deep into the myth and myself, I came to see how I had bought into my culture's silencing and repression of the female power inherent in the menstrual experience. It was a startling realization.

I am indebted to Áslaug Benediktsdóttir, Jórunn Tómasdóttir, Laurie Schapira, and Petah Digby, who put time and energy into reading and commenting on the draft of this book at its various stages. Their input and affirmations helped carry me along the way.

I felt lucky beyond words when Rachel Pollack accepted to edit my last draft before I submitted the manuscript to Chiron. Literally, it was a dream come true. Rachel had long been an inspiration for me through her approach to the Tarot. In her writings on the subject, I hear the wise womans' voice that is the object of my quest.

In 2013, I met Leonard Cruz, Editor-in-Chief at Chiron, at a Congress for Analytical Psychology in Copenhagen. That meeting turned out to be an encounter with Tyche, goddess of good fortune, whose name means "luck." Unknown to me then, this goddess who guards and protects, was introduced to me by Leonard Cruz in our first email exchange. This poetic opening of the process that lay ahead was a blessing that has stayed with me throughout. Working with Jennifer Fitzgerald, general manager of Chiron Publications, has been a joy. My thanks also go to copy editor Ronald Madden who helped shape up the manuscript, and to graphic designer Nelly Murariu for her splendid work on the appearance of the book.

I am deeply grateful to my analyst, Maxson J. McDowell, who has been my companion and guide on the inner journey in which this work is grounded; to Þorsteinn from Hamar for his inspiring poems; to Suzanne Carlile, through whom I obtained permission to include the "dream of a 13 year old American girl" in my work; and to that amazing, anonymous dreamer.

Last but not least, my profound gratitude goes to my husband, Herbert, for his loving support and unwavering belief in the eventual birth of this book.

Contents

Note to the reader

Translation of the tales and all quotes from Icelandic sources are by the author. Apart from "Thorn-Rose," the tales in this book are from *Icelandic Folk and Fairy Tales* collected by Jón Árnason (1819-1888). A common trait running through the tales in his collection is the storytellers' switching from the past to the present tense in moments of wonder and tension. Those inconsistencies are kept intact in the translation. Names of gods and goddesses are Anglicized whereas Icelandic orthography is maintained in the names of people and places, with the exception of the letters þ and ð which are rendered respectively as **th** and **d**.

"Thorn-Rose" is the one tale in this book that cannot be defined as Icelandic. Its roots, however, reach deep into the soil of the Icelandic people's Germanic ancestry. It thus forms an enlightening backdrop for the tales that follow. The tale as it appears here is my translation of Steingrímur Thorsteinsson's (1831-1913) rendition of *Dornröschen* in the *Book of Fairy Tales* that bears his name.

The *Prose Edda* by Snorri Sturluson (1179-1241) and the *Poetic Edda*, a collection of Old Norse poems, sometimes referred to as the *Elder Edda* (Ice. Eddukvæði), are the main sources for the mythological material which to a great extent informs the tales in this collection. *The Wise Wound: The Myths, Realities, and Meanings of Menstruation*, a pioneering book by Penelope Shuttle and Peter Redgrove, has been an important source for the hushed up female reality that is the main theme of this book.

Prelude

Dream of a 13-year-old American Girl
with permission of the dreamer

I am on a deserted beach that stretches out in every direction. Everything is gray. I'm on my knees on a sofa, looking over the side arm, and the tide is coming in, rolling under the sofa, then back out again. When it washes out I see a huge black snake slithering under the sofa in a figure eight. The tide keeps washing in and out, and the snake keeps swimming under the sofa. It's so big that the edges of the eight shape are sticking out from under the couch on all four sides. I am terrified of it and can't get off the couch. It seems like the dream was really long and this was all that happened in the whole thing, just the snake swimming over and over and me trapped on the couch.

This dream of a 13-year-old American girl was on the agenda of an online dream course in which I participated in 2011. We did however not have a chance to explore it due to lack of time. The dream had a profound impact on me and I sought permission from the anonymous dreamer to include it in my reflections on menstruation. I had the immediate feeling that in its stark simplicity the dream captured the essence of her culture's predicament in the face of this more or less outlawed part of every woman's life. The dreamer's terror was clear enough but it was only later that her posture, with its implied reverence, impressed itself on me. She is on her knees as she comes face to face with the impersonal power of nature. The permission was obtained through a third party as participants in the program did not bring in their own dreams but those of family and friends. So I did not have direct contact with the dreamer, but I did learn that she had dreamed the dream 20 years prior to its being brought to the group. This, it seems to me, is testimony to the deep impression it made on the dreamer.

Why did a dream of a 13-year-old trigger such a strong reaction in me, a woman in her mature years? In short, I was hit by the impersonal, deep-seated symbolism at its core. It felt as if her dream brought home the relevance of my journey through the tales of my ancestors and ancestresses which had taken me deep within myself and helped me see myself in the larger context of my cultural heritage. Here I was presented with the primal symbol of the snake, which figures in myths all over the world, emerging from the unconscious of a girl belonging to an era that we consider infinitely far removed from our mythological origins.

In my fantasy, the huge black snake washed upon the dreamer's shores right out of the Eden story, where the Biblical God put a curse on the woman and decreed an enmity between her and the snake. Much like the snake that slithers under the sofa in the girl's dream, this tale about humanity's loss of innocence due to disobedience has been an undercurrent in the Judeo-Christian mindset from time immemorial.

No doubt her dream speaks to the dreamer's present situation as dreams generally do. She seems to be on the threshold of a monumental experience that she fears and does not understand. Dreams also tend to exaggerate to emphasize and imprint their message if the conscious attitude of the dreamer makes too little of the issue they address. The repeated emphasis on the huge size of the snake would be a case in point. As the conscious attitude of a 13-year-old is likely to be largely influenced by her education and upbringing, the exaggerated aspect of her dream might be in response to the dismissive attitude of the collective to her situation. The universal aspect of the dream suggests to me that her experience is embedded in a larger context and as such is a reflection of the culture into which she was born. Her dream can therefore be moving as well as instructive for those of us who share that stage with her. Although she is all alone in her dream, her experience is in some sense universal.

In the context of the theme of this book, it is tempting to conjecture that the dreamer is on the threshold of womanhood. Her age and the symbolism of her dream would support such a conjecture. In the United States, the average age at menarche since the mid-1950s is 12 to 13 years. In Iceland it is 13 years. And so it was for me. An event vividly imprinted in my memory forever.

At this juncture, a girl's Eros starts to stir, the creative spark inherent in her nature, and that can be a frightening experience. In a sense it is a death experience, for the innocence of the child will give way to the awakening sexuality of the adult. Projecting my menstrual experience on the young girl's dream, I saw it as an outcry for guidance for the menarcheal girl in a culture that has demonized her flow and thus obstructed her access to her creative power. As I look back, I experience a sense of grief for not having been enlightened as to how I might have consciously engaged this aspect of myself.

In the dream the girl is alone between worlds, on the border of civilization (on a sofa) and nature, of land and the unfathomable sea. The horizontal figure eight embodied by the snake in her dream is, as explained by Paul Foster Case, an "ancient occult number ascribed to Hermes," a Greek god of transitions and boundaries.[1] The Roman god Mercury shared traits with Hermes to the extent that in the minds of men they came to designate the same mythical

---

1   1947. *The Tarot: A Key to the Wisdom of the Ages*, pp. 41-42.

being. Both were seen as messengers of the gods and as such they were bringers of dreams. To the explanation quoted above Case adds: "This horizontal eight is also a symbol of the Holy Spirit." Mercury became an important ingredient for the medieval alchemists, both as substance, i.e. fluid quicksilver, and symbol. Alchemy was the forerunner of modern chemistry and the alchemists believed they could transform base metals into gold in their laboratories. But Carl Jung, who found support for his theory of individuation in their writings, discovered that the ultimate goal of their endeavor, even if to an extent unconscious, was to transform their instincts, their base nature, into spiritual gold.

Looked at from this angle, the young girl's initiatory dream could be seen as a display of precious creative potential. To realize her potential, she will need to muster the courage to face and accept her wild serpent nature and channel it into creative acts. At the time of the dream, she felt cornered, trapped on the sofa, but if she stays true to herself she will eventually find a way out of her entrapment. Even if she did not understand her dream at the time, it will continue to live and evolve within her like the foetus in the womb and push her ever closer towards the goal of its fulfilment. This can be a lifelong process.

The Tarot card attributed to Strength and the number eight (see image[2]) might be relevant to the young girl's dream. As do myths and dreams, Tarot cards display universal images which mirror human potential and can form a bridge to our authentic selves. The Strength card shows a woman taming a lion that seemingly stands for her instinctual fiery nature. She is clad in white which I take to denote the purity of her intention. This tells me that she does not attempt to circumvent or repress her nature but attunes herself to

---

2   My drawings are based on Pamela Coleman Smith's images on the Rider-Waite-Smith tarot cards, published in 1909.

VIII

STRENGTH

it, like a musician playing her instrument. She gently controls but does not close the animal's mouth. In fact, in some decks she opens it wide as if to give voice to the unadulterated truths of nature. Her hold on the devouring mouth further emphasizes that she does not let herself be swallowed by her fears and passions. Rather she draws strength from her animal nature. The transformation of animal fire into a garland and crown of roses is telling of her blossoming creativity. And over her head hovers the black snake that the 13-year-old encountered in her dream.

In addition to the symbolism quoted from Case above, the black horizontal eight is a sign of infinity called *lemniscate*. This symbolism accords with the sense of infinity that seems to be embedded in the dream experience and with the incessant flux and reflux of the tide, as it does also with the waxing and waning of the moon. The dream seems to hold up to the dreamer the eternal rhythm of the universe which she needs to be attuned to in order to function as a creative individual.

In the system of Tarot, each Major Arcana card is associated with a Hebrew letter and interestingly the one attributed to Strength, *Teth*, means "snake." In the words of Case, it is a "symbol of what has been known among occultists for ages as the 'serpent-power.'"[3] This could be useful information for a young girl who is terrified of the power that resides in her. Instead of feeling trapped in her feminine nature as victim of the monthly "curse," a woman who is receptive to the instinctual wisdom of the menstrual energy embarks upon a creative adventure in the service of evolution. Whereas the woman in Major Arcana card number Eight draws Strength from animal instinct, the Tarot Magician (see image) seemingly channels energy from above. The card is an expression of the Hermetic dictum "as above, so below" and shows the Magician as a mediator between

---

3   Ibid., p. 103.

THE MAGICIAN

heaven and earth, between spirit and embodied existence. In both instances the *lemniscate*, the horizonal number eight, hovers above the protagonist's head which we tend to identify as the seat of human intellect. In other words, the wisdom inherent in this symbol is shown to be of a higher order.

Why do we have a female protagonist on the former card and a male on the latter? This has not to do with gender but with different manifestations of the one energy that pervades the universe. Astrologically Strength is associated with the planet Leo and the element Fire but the Magician is associated with the planet Mercury and the element Air. Fire spells passions and Air is mental. The depictions on the cards would seem to reflect the ingrained cultural stereotypes that women are closer to the animal and men are more mental. The Rider-Waite-Smith Tarot cards, on which these drawings are based, were published in 1909. Now is another era. With women outnumbering men in universities around the world, this tenacious prejudice is being laid to rest. The energies reflected on these cards are beyond gender distinction and belong to both women and men.

So the Magician, too, could be key to the possibilities of the menarcheal girl. The Magician is an instrument of a will superior to his own. The same could be said about the menstruating woman who has no saying over her flow, that is, if she does not resort to pharmaceutical means. As the Magician, she would be a mediatrix in the service of Creation and hence a co-creator. The tools at her disposal, depicted on the Magician's table, are the four elements that the world—man as microcosm and the universe as macrocosm— was believed to be composed of: water (cup), fire (staff), air (sword), and earth (pentacle). What is aimed for is a harmonious whole, an attunement to the symphony of the universe of which our dreamer is a living part.

I

An Unexpected Gift

was drawn to the theme of menstruation by a dream. In this
dream, I was presented with a silver necklace by an admired poet:

*I am in the crowded cafeteria at the university. Thorsteinn from
Hamar (the poet) stands behind the counter. I ask for a cup of coffee. In
addition to my order he puts out a plate with a slice of poundcake, on
top of which is placed a silver key ring. I ask how much I owe and hand
him a (red) note of five hundred crowns. "One hundred," he responds
and takes the change of four hundred out of the register. I would have
thought I should pay more, that the coffee alone was a hundred. "In
that case I have the exact amount," I say and pull a (green) note of
one hundred crowns from my wallet. He gives me back the note of five*

hundred. I pick up the silver key ring and hand it back to him. But he says no, he wants to give it to me. I am speechless. I don't feel that I can accept it. "And I who never give you anything," he says. He then takes out a silver necklace and gives it to me. I am filled with joy as I walk back to the table, but I don't show my gifts. I hope that Thorsteinn won't feel bad about that...

In retrospect, I believe it was Thorsteinn's preoccupation with silence—the "silent, hidden, archaic, behind all that is..."—that held me captive. I had studied his poems at the university where the teacher challenged us with the question, "What is this silence he is talking about?" No one ventured forth with an answer. Wisely, the teacher left it at that. But by asking, he had planted a seed. The correlation between the theme of silence and menstruation is clear to me now, but at the time of the dream my focus was on the necklace. As my dream poet also gave me a silver key ring, I knew it was my task to find the key. And so I was propelled on a quest.

My immediate association was to Freyja's necklace, Brísingamen. I felt a deep affinity with this goddess of love and fertility and was in particular fascinated by her aspect as *völva* ("wise woman" and "seeress") whose voice had at some point been silenced. I felt it was an urgent ethical issue to acknowledge and restore the feminine wisdom incarnated by the *völva*. And so the poet's gift dwelt within me like a promise which I knew it was my duty to fulfill. But as is the case with some of the heroines in the tales of this collection, I did not dare acknowledge that I was worthy of the favor bestowed on me by a poet whom I so admired. I cherished the gift in secret but could not claim it openly as mine. Sixteen years would pass before I felt the impulse to send a poem in to a competition. When I got a call announcing that my poem had won, it felt like a natural fulfilment of the dream.

Years after I had the dream, I was invited to write about Freyja for a dictionary of symbols, and that was when I discovered the key to Brísingamen and its relationship with menstruation. It felt like a momentous breakthrough. The key, I found out, is in the name, which conjoins the opposites of fire and the (frosty) moon. *Brísingr* means "fire" and *men* derives from the moon root *men*. Scholars have struggled, without conclusive results, to unveil the meaning of the legendary object and reconstruct the myth behind it from scattered fragments. The only coherent description of Freyja's acquisition of the necklace, and its subsequent theft at Odin's behest by the trickster Loki, is to be found in a manuscript from the end of the fourteenth century, written and compiled by two Catholic priests. The tale is told with grotesque humor and presents the old gods and goddesses as mortal beings whose mythical abode, Asgard, is placed in exotic and faraway Asia. Fragments from older texts suggest, however, that the roots of the tale reach far into the past. Following are excerpts from my text about Freyja based on this tale:

> She comes to a stone and finds that it is open. It turns out to be the smithy of four dwarfs who are forging a gold necklace. She is attracted to it, starts to negotiate, she wants it. Taken by her beauty, the dwarfs will let her have it only if she spends one night with each. She surrenders herself and emerges with the treasure.[1]

In a flash of insight, I saw the image of a solar eclipse in this ancient symbol, the union of the heavenly bodies of the sun and the moon brought down to earth:

> As in Norse mythology Sun is feminine and Moon masculine, Freyja's adventure conjures up an image of the descending sun who abandons herself in the dissolving embrace of the moon in its dark phase, her red embers bleeding from under his coal-black disk, arranged in a flaming necklace.

Eventually, I came to understand the myth about Freyja's acquisition of Brísingamen as a tale of initiation, of the first flow as

---

1   This is my retelling of Freyja's acquisition of the necklace, based on "Sörla þáttr" in *Fornaldar sögur Norðurlanda*, I. My text about Freyja was written for ARAS (Archive for Research in Archetypal Symbolism) and is posted on my website www.dreamsandtarot.is.

envisioned at the dawn of day by our ancestresses who recognized their own experience in the celestial union. In traditional society, every time something new comes into being, there is a creation myth behind it. And so, I imagine that when a girl went through the transition from child to woman, the original episode, cast in the mold of Freyja's experience, was reenacted in a ritual and symbolic way. In this manner, Brísingamen would have been passed down from one generation of women to the next until it was stolen by Odin, the god of warlords.

From the perspective of Jungian analysis, a dream holds up to the dreamer a process that has already run its course but may take the individual a lifetime to work through. In like manner, Freyja's going down to the underworld to acquire the gold necklace reflects the potential to reach the spiritual perfection symbolized by the gold. This potential is inherent in her human daugthers who, if receptive of the gift bestowed on them, come closer to the goal with each cycle. Cyclicity is also reflected in the necklace which is frequently represented as a gold ring. Freyja's example would have been a guiding light for a girl going through a rebirth experience, holding out the promise of a precious reward. Going down into the mineral world means going deep into matter, deep into the body. It is an approach that runs counter to the Christian yearning for Heaven and counter to the fear of the sinful body. Hence "going into rocks" came to be seen as an engagement with evil as will be exemplified in the tales that follow.

I had my first period around the time of my confirmation at age 13. Both occasions marked my entry into adulthood, both are vividly imprinted in my memory. There was, however, no connecting link between the two in my mind. The official confirmation of my entry into the community of adults was the partaking of the bread and the wine at the altar, the body and blood of Christ who had suffered and died on the cross for our sins. It was a true test, for I feared that I would bring disgrace on myself for not being able to get the wine and the pale, tasteless cookie down. This had been a common apprehension amongst us girls, and we had to avoid looking at each other in order not to burst out laughing. The passion and bloodshed of Christ was totally obfuscated by our effort to keep a solemn and serious face. The hushed up bleeding from our own bodies was a more immediate preoccupation at this time in our lives.

I was attending a sewing club with my playmates when menstruation crept in on me. Our weekly meetings devoted to needlework or knitting were modeled on our mothers' sewing clubs. In the community where I grew up, most women belonged to one. We had started the evening by making a compote of sorrel, picked on the moor below our street. It turned out to be a delicacy that we served proudly with sugar and cream. We were carefree kids playing at being adults, all in a hurry to grow up and become masters of our own lives.

I am embroidering brightly colored animals on a pen case. There is laughter and well-being in the air. Then it happened. All of a sudden I notice a dull ache spread over my lower back, like a sense of fatigue. I instantly knew. I feel weighted down, as if I am being torn apart at the waist. I sit silent for a while and tune into the unfamiliar sensation. Then I notify my friends. Filled with anticipation, we file into the toilet. There is suspense in the air. I have never seen menstrual blood before and... I stare in disbelief at the brown stain in my white panties. "You have begun!" my friends twitter, awe and excitement written on their faces.

The following day, I am circling around my mother who is adjusting her beautiful auburn hair in front of the mirror. "You know," she says, fixing her face in the glass, "now you have to beware of boys." That was all. My mother, who bore the name[2] of the sacred

---

2   *Ragnheidur* is a composite word, the first part of which refers to the gods or divine powers while the latter part, *heidur*, was a name given to *völvas* in the old sagas. A völva or **völva** is a shamanic seeress and a recurring motif in Norse mythology.

völva, "seer and prophetess," had forgotten that the first bleeding does not signify solely that a girl's womb has become fertile soil for the seed of a man. She had forgotten that her blood is the fertilizer that nourishes her roots and promotes her growth.

As I look back on my crossing over into womanhood, it feels like an oracular beginning. In the ancient tales, the bower—where women devoted themselves to sewing, weaving, song, poetry, and dreaming—is a place of mystery. As we will see in the tales, it was a place that males could only steal a peek into through a slit in the roof or a not too transparent window. I wonder whether male secret orders, such as the Freemasons, did not spring up in response to that secluded place of female mystery. And what about those traditional gentlemen's clubs, some of which still do not open their doors to women? Could their roots be traced to men's endeavor to turn the tables on the women who in the distant past excluded them from their bowers?

In the tale about Freyja and the dwarfs, Freyja's sovereignty over her bower is emphasized:

> She had her own bower. She was both beautiful and strong, so that it is said that if the door was closed and locked, no man was allowed into the bower without Freyja's consent.[3]

Immediately after this passage follows, like a dream, the account of Freyja's descent into the stone where she sleeps with the four dwarfs for four nights and returns to her bower with her gold necklace. It is my belief that Freyja's necklace is fundamentally an image of the bleeding vulva, of the *red-gold* lacing the neck of the womb.

It is important to keep in mind that this tale was committed to vellum by Christian priests, who introduced Freyja as a mortal and as Odin's concubine and then went on to show her pay with

---

3   "Sörla þáttr" in *Fornaldar sögur Norðurlanda*, I, p. 367.

sex for a necklace that she covets. In other words, she is portrayed as a woman of loose morals and a whore, but she is also strong and independent. It seems safe to conclude that Freyja did not conform to patriarchy's idea of a faithful and subordinate wife. When I turned to this text in search of a key to my dream about the silver necklace, I was disconcerted. It felt like a personal attack. All I could see was the defilement of something I knew in my heart was sacred. I was enraged at the priests' trespassing on holy ground and their mocking of the goddess. My anger became a driving force. I was not about to let them taint my dream poet's gift, which I felt was connected to the goddess's necklace in some deep and meaningful way.

I had finished the manuscript of this book when I came upon a quote in Jung's *Psychology and Alchemy*, which threw a bright light on the priests' portrayal of Freyja and the reason why Odin coveted her necklace. In this quote, offered by Jung in a footnote, Eirenaeus Philalethes, a renowned 17th century alchemist, claims that the alchemists knew how to "extract the Royal Diadem from the menstrual blood of a whore."[4] This metaphor was a find that supported my feeling that there is a strong alchemical undercurrent in our mythological material. And it fit beautifully into the picture of Freyja that I had attempted to piece together from the glimpses we get of her in the myths.

---

4 "For there are in our initial material many superfluities of various kinds which can never be reduced to purity. Therefore it is advantageous to wash them all out thoroughly, but this cannot be done without the *theoria* of our secrets, in which we give instructions for extracting the Royal Diadem from the menstruum of a whore" (note 3, par. 403). Jung is expounding the alchemists' idea of *theoria* but does not address the striking metaphor of "the menstruum of a whore." *Menstruum* means "solvent" or "menstrual discharge" and is so defined by *The Free Dictionary*: "From Medieval Latin, from Latin *mēnstruus* monthly, from *mēnsis* month; from an alchemical comparison between base metal being transmuted into gold and the supposed action of the menses" (http://www.thefreedictionary.com/menstruum). In *"Decknamen or pseudochemical language"? Eirenaeus Philalethes and Carl Jung* by William R. Newman, the substance is spelled out in plain terms as "the menstrual blood of our whore" or even of a "sordid whore" (http://www.persee.fr/web/revues/home/prescript/article/rhs_0151-4105_1996_num_49_2_1254), pp. 181-182.

In the "Prelude," I touched on the parallel that Jung saw between the alchemical procedure and his work as a psychoanalyst. He came to the understanding that the alchemists projected their inner processes on the experiments they were performing in their laboratories. What they were ultimately seeking, Jung concluded, was their own immortal essence to which they referred as the *lapis* or the philosopher's stone. By the same token, his analysands would work their way toward wholeness by recognizing and accepting unknown parts of themselves, which they had projected outside of themselves. In other words, the goal of therapeutic work is to withdraw projections and own them.

Freyja might be seen as a guiding example in this respect. She wants to *own* the necklace that she sees in the stone. She wants to own her menstrual nature, and she is prepared to pay for it with gold and silver and precious objects. But the dwarfs decline her offers and only want her to lie one night with each of them. She surrenders herself and obtains the treasure. As menstruation is a natural occurrence, we might ask; Why did she have to pay for it? The answer is that she saw value in it, and as Jung has pointed out, the unconscious is unwilling to let anything outside its magical circle without a sacrifice of some sort. What Freyja sacrificed was in essence herself; for in the transition from child to woman, a girl goes through a death and rebirth experience. By following Freyja's example and embracing her nature, the menstruating woman is rewarded with transforming wisdom and an intimate knowledge of nature. Freyja's example indicates that there is mutual gain for the conscious self and the unconscious in this exchange. In other words, the revelations the unconscious transmits to the woman are to be used in the service of evolution. Odin's theft of Freyja's necklace is a testament to the male endeavor to gain control over the blood that, in the last analysis, transcends man's will. Freyja shows us the way of the feminine as opposed to the heroic masculine, whose thieving and aggressive exploitation of nature has gained the upper hand in the ways of the world.

As explained by Jung, a prerequisite for the inception of the alchemical work is to find the raw material to work with, the *prima materia* or "initial material" to which Philalethes refers as "the menstrual blood of a whore." This is, however, no easy matter for it tends to be something that we do not want to see as belonging to ourselves, "the most despised and rejected thing, 'thrown into the street,' 'cast on the dunghill,' 'found in the filth.'"[5] After all, what is more despised and rejected in patriarchal culture than *menstruation* and a *whore?* In this "lowly" matter, projected onto the feminine, lay dormant the seed of the highest good that for Philalethes and the alchemists was the Royal Diadem. It is ironic that man's raw material for the Great Work, the alchemical Opus, was projected on the most intimate female nature while a great many women have turned their back on the natural power invested in them. The theft of Freyja's necklace by Odin, a patriarchal god, suggests that at some point in time men usurped women's power and turned it against them. The tales that follow give us an insight into this reality. Their menses, once considered a precious gift, became a curse and a nuisance.

The alchemists' spiritual endeavors, Jung concludes, "is a process of coming to terms with the unconscious, which always sets in when man is confronted with its darkness. This confrontation forced itself on the alchemist as soon as he made a serious effort to find the prima materia."[6] From both Jung's definition, and my own feeling, I deduce that it was no accident that I was propelled on my quest by a dream, which held up to me the alluring image of a silver necklace given to me by a poet. The dream, I came to realize, was a compensation for my conscious attitude, which was to a great extent forged by my schooling under the auspices of patriarchal culture. The scholars who had laid the foundation for the understanding of our cultural heritage were exclusively male. I was an eager student

5   1967, par. 209.

6   Ibid.

and applied myself to assimilating the material presented to me, but something was amiss. In spite of my good grades, I felt inadequate. And I kept trying to find firm footing through more studies and more studies, till my dream emerged from deep within and brought up precious stuff that led me on to the *prima materia*. When I had discovered the key to my dream in the theme of menstruation, I could begin to understand the dissolving processes mirrored in my dreams as my old and hardened ways gradually crumbled to give way to a new sense of self. Sometimes I would be menstruating in a dream and reliving the physical sensation that accompanied the flow, despite the fact that I was well past that phase in my life. It became clear to me that I needed to get in touch with my lunar nature in order to find roots in myself; it also became clear that Brísingamen was the key of admittance.

The echo of Freyja's "bridal episode" in the stone reverberates through the tales in this collection. This suggests to me that it represents repressed material that seeks to get out into the light of day. By virtue of its name, Brísingamen conjoins the opposites of solar and lunar energies. Indications of the belief that menstrual bleeding was caused by the moon having intercourse with the woman are to be found far and wide.[7] This would typically have happened at the new moon when its luminous body disappears from the sky and is said to be conjunct with the sun. The tale emphasizes that the dwarfs were in the process of forging the necklace when Freyja came to the stone and that it was about to be finished. This suggests that Freyja—avatar of the sun as goddess of love and fertility—goes underground and unites with her lunar lover in the moon's last and

---

7   See for instance Shuttle and Redgrove, who give examples of the belief that the moon is "the dream or 'other husband' of the woman, and has sexual intercourse with her at the period." They also quote a recent study by Herz and Jensen in which menstruating women are "[...] shown to be more preoccupied with male adult figures, other than husbands and fathers, in their dreams then than at other times" (pp. 98-99). The tale, "Katla's Dream," is an illustration of this (Chapter 5 in this book).

dark phase, which gives birth to the luminous crescent moon. As night goes before day, this is the place of beginnings and endings.

The dwarfs' desire for Freyja is emphasized. The tale echoes a theme found in legends that the "Man in the Moon" has a lustful attraction to all females.[8] The conception of the moon as a man, who is believed to be the cause of menstruation, is said to be found among primitive peoples in various places of the world.[9] And certain tribal communities reportedly regard him as a lecherous male seeking to deflower young girls and thus causing the onset of their menstruation.[10] In line with this belief is the rumor reported by one scholar that Brísingamen was made for Freyja by the dwarfs "at the expense of her chastity."[11] In our Western culture, a woman is considered to be an unblemished virgin until she has had sexual intercourse with a mortal man. Not so for the Kumari girls in Nepal who are worshipped as incarnations of the goddess Taleju, that is, until they start to menstruate. Then it is believed that the goddess leaves their body. As Kumari means "virgin," and purity is a central issue in this tradition, it is implied that at menarche a girl loses her virginity.

One has to wonder where this widespread belief of woman's intimate relations with the moon came from. Does it suggest that when attuned to their lunar nature women's experience of the flow was erotic? Could the bleeding caused by the rupture of the hymen

---

8   *Man, Myth & Magic.* Vol. 14, p. 1877: "In a number of legends the moon is regarded as male, and the 'Man in the Moon' is said to have lustful attraction to all females."

9   *Encyclopaedia Britannica.* "Nature Worship" in Macropeadia 12, p. 880: "The conception of the moon as a man (who frequently is believed to be the cause of menstruation) among primitive hunter peoples (African Bushmen, Australian Aborigines, and hunters of South America) and among certain pastoral and royal cultures of Africa (*e.g.,* the Masai and the Hottentots)."

10   *Man, Myth & Magic.* Vol. 14, p. 1877: "Among certain tribal communities the moon is [...] regarded as a lecherous male who roams the earth, especialy during the bright nights of the full moon, seeking whom he may deflower. He succeeds in ravishing every single maiden on earth, and the token of his success is the phenomenon of menstruation."

11   Magnus Magnusson, p. 76.

on what would ideally be a woman's wedding night have triggered the belief that menarche was brought about by an invisible bridegroom? Or did the tabooed menstruating woman exert an attraction that was projected on the "Man in the Moon?" Odin's reaction to the means by which Freyja obtained her jewel seems to suggest as much.

Seclusion of the menstruating woman has been widely practiced since time immemorial, be it in a special outhouse or a dark corner of the house. Menstrual seclusion is generally held to have been forced upon woman by man because she was unclean. The above description of Freyja's sovereignty over her bower that no man was allowed to enter without her consent, however, accords with the emerging view that ritual seclusion may have been initiated by the women themselves.[12] Attuned to the lunar rhythm, they would withdraw to their bower when the moon withdrew from the sky, either by themselves or in groups, and devote themselves to spiritual and creative tasks. This is corroborated by glimpses we get into the bower from the old sagas and tales. The emphasis on Freyja's strength when it came to securing privacy in her bower intimates that women had to defend their sovereignty over their body.

When I had the dream about the poet and the silver necklace, I had been through a surgically induced menopause due to fibroids and heavy bleedings. Hysterectomy was a matter of course. The gynecologist who was to perform the operation announced that *he* was going to remove, not only my uterus, but also the ovaries and cervix to prevent me from getting cancer later on. It was a

---

12   To quote George Elder in the ARAS Encyclopedia *The Body*: "Scholars have begun to suggest that the 'ritual isolation' of menstruating women may have originated among women who long ago noticed the concordance of their periods with the periodic phases of the moon, women who watched that heavenly body wax and wane and felt their own energies naturally come and go." He suggests that ritual periods of isolation would have served "to ponder the mysteries of sacred nature, privately or in groups" (p. 305). And Shuttle and Redgrove: "In some cultures [...] these customs of seclusion, which may at first have been adopted by the women for their own benefit, to take advantage of a 'moment of truth' in their bodies, have hardened into cruel and stereotyped practices" (p. 76).

moment of truth for me. I was struck by the analogy between the mythical heroes' rapacious invasions into the womb of mother earth and the medical institution's aggressive attitude towards women's reproductive organs. I was reminded of Odin's deceitful entry into Gunnlöd's rock and his theft of the vessel containing the mead of poetry that was under her guardianship. It was a deed, lauded in myths and by scholars that I had not been able to forgive. I knew that surgeons are paid in relation to the organ(s) they remove. Mindful of the old myths, I now wondered whether my womb had become a gold mine under the pretext of a noble deed! I was put up against a choice: if I were to get cancer, I would have myself to blame for it. In spite of my inhibiting fear of such a fate, I decided to shoulder the responsibility. I found another doctor and kept my sound organs. I cannot help but wonder if negative expectations of this sort that are disguised as prophylaxis against future cancer do not pave the way for the very disease the medical institution endeavors to prevent.

The search for the key to my dream took me back in time, not only to my personal memories of menstruation, but also to the collective experiences of my foremothers that I gleaned from myths, fairy tales, and folk tales. An in-depth study of this material revealed to me the repression of the wisdom and healing potential inherent in the menstrual experience. It was as if I were given a second chance to consciously live an experience that I had missed out on during my fertile years. What stood out in my memory was a certain intimacy with myself during the period as my focus was pulled down into my body. This feeling was now brought up again in dream encounters, gentle and caressing, with my dream poet. Having come to realize that people who appear in my dreams frequently stand for qualities that I have not embraced or claimed in myself, I eventually understood that the poet represented my desire, my need really, to connect to the poet in myself.

Freyja's husband Od (Óðr) is but a name in the myths. The word's primary meaning is "poetry," "poem." As an adjective it refers to the "wild" nature of Freyja's soulmate. That is to say, the name refers simultaneously to the raw material of a poem and the perfected poem itself. I take it to mean that the seed of poetry is hidden in wild nature. As told by Snorri Sturluson:

> She [Freyja] married a man named Od. Their daughter is Hnoss. She is so beautiful that that which is beautiful and precious is called "hnoss" after her. Od went far away, but Freyja stays behind and cries, but her tear is red-gold.[13]

In the poem *Völuspá* ("Prophecy of the Seeress"), *óðr* is the noun for "soul" or, as phrased by one scholar, "the 'divine spark' in man which is influenced by higher powers."[14] The name of Freyja's hidden or absent husband suggests a wild spirit whose territory lies outside civilization. That wildness is inherent in the menstrual flow over which even a king like Sleeping Beauty's father wields no power. Od, as I see it, is Freyja's divine inspiration, her muse. He is her "dream husband."[15]

Paula Weideger points out that in "the reality defined by a man's world" woman's "weeping womb, and menstruation" are described "as the failure of conception."[16]. This view, it seems to me, makes of motherhood a duty that the menstruating woman fails to fulfil. The object of Freyja's sorrow is Od, for whom she searches "amongst foreign peoples" while assuming various names and guises. She is driven by desire for the union with her divine other. In her daughter Hnoss, begotten by Od and whose name means "treasure," I see a symbolic representation of Freyja's rebirth as she reappears fertile and cleansed from her menstrual seclusion, as well as her rebirth in her menarcheal daughters, daughters like Thorunn in the tale

---

13 "Gylfaginning," ch. 35.

14 Nordal, p. 73.

15 I refer again to Shuttle and Redgrove (pp. 98-99) as pr. note 4 above.

16 P. 140.

of "The 'Hidden Woman' in Hafnanúpur," who sadly failed to accept her inherited gift (Chapter 4). As is implied by Hnoss's name, Freyja's offspring was conceived of as "the treasure hard to get" and object of the hero's quest in myths and fairy tales, frequently under the pretext of freeing the helpless maiden from the grips of evil.

Before describing Freyja's strength and sovereignty over her bower and her subsequent descent into the stone, the tale emphasizes Odin's love for her. He was less than happy with how she obtained her necklace and expedited Loki on a mission to steal it from her. He agreed to return it on the condition that she instigate a war between two kings that was to last until a Christian succeeded in bringing the feud to an end. Freyja gave her consent and reclaimed her necklace.

As a consequence of this shady deal, woman was thrown into conflict with herself. This struggle is portrayed in the saga by placing *Hild*, whose name means "battle," in a grove from which she looks upon her father and her husband, who both have a place in her heart, in fierce battle along with their armies. No sooner did they split each other from head to shoulder than they rose again and continued fighting. At last, after a 143 years, they were released from the curse by the courtier of a Christian king. The humorous overtones with which the Christian priests related this human drama projected on the heathen gods and goddesses are wrought with overbearing vis-à-vis the pre-Christian mindset. Counter to its unifying nature, Brísingamen, or rather the woman who embodied its divine essence, now became a bone of contention between two superhuman powers cast in the images of the lunar divinity and Odin, and I dare say for very different reasons. Her relationship with the former was an alliance in the service of growth and evolution on the collective plane while the latter strove to take control of her nature and usurp it to his end. In a nutshell, woman was caught between the old order of the agricultural ancestors, whose lives were attuned to the cyclicity inherent in nature, and a new order of warlords who endeavored to conquer nature on all fronts—not the least of which was woman's menstrual nature—which was decried as monstrous.[17] Accordingly, when Freyja had fulfilled Odin's wish to sow the seed of enmity between the two kings, she faded from the scene, huge and black. Her name on this infamous mission was *Göndul*, which means "she who carries a staff." As the staff was an attribute of the *völva*, this is a clear reference to the *völva*-aspect of Freyja.

At the heart of this succinct and irreverent tale is the takeover by the male god of woman's menstrual nature in the service of division and war and a defamation of the *völva* as a medium for the unadulterated voice of nature. In the guise of Göndul, she is a mouthpiece for Odin and his devious plans. It is also emphasized that Freyja gives in to Odin's conditions without the slightest resistance. The *men* is all-important for her. I suspect that there is a play on the word *men* here which in Icelandic means both a "necklace" (neck-ring) and a "pendant" (locket). In the light of the origin of Freyja's Brísinga*men* as described in this tale, that is, her sexual union with the dwarfs, the latter meaning could be intended as a *sub rosa* reference to the male genitalia and Freyja's thirst for sex, which gives Odin power over her. This is a familiar enough theme that rings through the Lord's decree to "the woman" in which he makes it clear that her desire shall be for her husband and that he shall rule over her.[18] But as it is *Freyja's jewel* that is the central issue here, this doubleentendre would more logically refer to the goddess's "phallic" side, which has been shown to express itself at the menstrual pole of a woman's lunar cycle (cf., "The Hermaphroditic Rose" in Chapter 3).

The rhythmic relationship between the female menstrual cycle and the moon has been recognized from the dawn of time. Our

---

17 In "Menstruating Female Figure," George R. Elder introduces this quote from Pliny: "But to come again to women hardly can there be found anything more monstrous than is that flux and course of theirs" (p. 305).

18 Gen. 3:16.

agricultural ancestors lived by the lunar calendar, counting 13 moons in a year, thus standing in accord with the 13 menstrual periods of an unimpregnated woman. The lunar calendar was later replaced by the 12 months of the solar year. In her enlightening interpretation of "Sleeping Beauty," where the irate 13th fairy is left out because the king has only 12 gold plates, Annette Høst addresses the conflict caused by this transition.[19]

As opposed to Freyja's surrender to her lunar nature which graced her with an incomparable treasure, the onset of menstruation in the tales that follow is brought about by the intrusion or rape of forces that are perceived as hostile. The one exception is the pastor's wife in "The Witch's Ride," who heeds the call of the blood in her quest for knowledge but is subjected to deserved punishment for consorting with the Devil. When my eyes had opened to the menstrual meaning of Brísingamen, I was dumbfounded to discover that in the six volumes of *Icelandic Folk and Fairy Tales* there is but this one disparaging story that deals with menstruation in plain terms. How was it possible that such an important part of a woman's life was so completely overlooked? The question I should have asked was, why had I not noticed the silence shrouding this issue before? Yet I had participated in this hiding game, worrying that I would be exposed in public by a stain of blood on my behind. I had never stopped to ask myself why that would have been so shameful, given that I had no control over the flow.

But what of the silver necklace and key ring given to me by a poet, symbolic dream images that have led me to this project? It has occurred to me that woman goes through a second initiation during menopause, this time into her cronehood. In fairy tales as well as in traditional societies, the crone is a teacher and a guide for younger

---

19   "Blessed by the Moon" on http://www.shamanism.dk.

women. If the message of the dream was about my initiation into cronehood, the dream presented me in a role that I needed to grow out of, that of a student. The staging of my dream was in the cafeteria at the university. I was a student and the poet a vendor or salesclerk. In retrospect I realize that I was so preoccupied with the gift and the giver that I paid no attention to the setting, which is highly relevant in a dream. By putting the poet, for whom I had such a lofty admiration, in the role of a servant, the dream brought him down to earth and by so doing made my inner poet more accessible for me. If that was the goal of the dream all along, to bring the poet out into the open, I had to find my way back to the stone in which Freyja acquired her necklace and surrender my narrow sense of self to an authority of a higher order than the ruling powers of the culture into which I was born. I can only hope that by sharing that journey, I will in some small way realize my role as a crone.

My drawings became an important part of the search for self, allowing me to experience an all but forgotten childlike joy. Again the seed was planted by a dream in which I was lost in drawing one picture after another without the slightest concern for what the world might think of them. I felt the pull, but it seemed like an absurd waste of time. I was convinced that I could not draw, although I have frequently asked myself why, at a given moment, I had put this delightful activity of my childhood on the shelf for good. Clearly I did not have the talent of an artist, and as we are taught to excel, I put my energy into more serious endeavors condoned by the educational establishment. But maybe it was precisely the fact that I did not have to prove myself that enabled me to lose myself in sheer bliss. And through losing myself, I found a lost part of myself.

2
Background
Personal and Collective

I experience fairy tales and folk tales as a living substance that deepens my understanding of myself and of human nature in general. In childhood, these stories held a particular fascination for me. My father had a big and heavy book with impressive illustrations by some of our most celebrated artists whose creative imagination had been stirred by these tales. I passed this book in tatters on to my son. He, too, fell for its magic. I can still remember being swept along deep into the story. The risk and the tension felt real and exhilarating. I sided with the hero in every test, was shot through with relief when the giantesses were unmasked, and applauded their gruesome death. I saw nothing wrong with the retribution dealt the false queen in "The Giantess on the Stoneboat" (Chapter 8). You may remember that the king had a hood pulled over her head before she was stoned and attached to wild horses that tore her asunder. If only the "hidden" woman (as we Icelanders call those nature beings whom most of us cannot see with our mortal eyes) in the folktale "The 'Hidden Woman' in Hafnanúpur" had had her head covered, Thorunn, the protagonist of the story, would not have become the victim of her evil eye (Chapter 4). I was inoculated with the virtues a good girl should strive for. Thorunn and her likes were ideals held up to young females. Loved and cherished by all, they had everything a man could ask for in a wife. But even if Thorunn was gentleness incarnated, she met with ill fortune. Now I wonder whether the curse that befell her was not caused by the virginal ideal imposed on her by the spirit of her times, for certainly Thorunn was much bigger than the succinct and lofty description of her personality would have us believe. But this I did not understand when I was a child.

To the adult reader, Thorunn's story shows in a clear light that it is our attitude toward nature that determines whether we experience it as benevolent or malevolent. At first sight, she feels that the "hidden woman" looks out to her with a friendly mien but when fear takes hold of her, the woman in the mount turns into a noxious being. Nature itself is neutral.

Now someone might ask why I feel driven to dig into this legacy. My tenacious interest is rooted in the personal experience I elaborated on in the previous chapter, a dream in which a poet gave me a silver key ring and a silver necklace. The dream led me on the track of Freyja's legendary necklace, Brísingamen. As I explained, my vision of Freyja's gold necklace is that of the bleeding vulva, of the *red-gold* lacing the neck of the womb. Old sources, reaching as far back as the 9th century, refer to the theft of Brísingamen. The very fact that it was stolen hints at its value. It also suggests that it was an emblem of power that the ruling powers coveted but felt that women needed to be dispossessed of.

The repression of menstrual power due to its demonization in patriarchal culture jumps to the eyes of anyone willing to see. Fairy tales and folk tales tend to expose the underside of the cultural situation in which they emerge. I consider this shadow stuff to be part of my heritage. If my ancestors did not deal with a vital issue in a satisfactory manner, its shadow side continues to live in me. As it found its way into the ancestral tales, it is likely to surface in my dreams, given the opportune circumstances, and to solicit my understanding and cooperation. It is from this standpoint that I approach the seven tales that have accrued around the theme that runs through my interpretation. They have helped me shed light, not solely on my own psychological struggles, but also on the predicament of the culture to which I belong. Thus my interpretation addresses both the personal and the collective. While I may refer to scholars who have added to or support my understanding of the material, I want to emphasize that my approach to the stories is above all personal and that I take the liberty to have imagination as my companion on this journey. But first let us take a closer look at what prompted the quest.

Shortly before the dream about the poet and the necklace, I had finished my M.A. thesis in Icelandic literature in which I dealt with my mythological heritage from the viewpoint of Jungian psychology. I am indebted to my mentor for suggesting Jung to me. Apart from a cursory introduction into his theory of the archetypes, I knew very little about him. As studies in Jung were not offered at the university at the time nor was there a Jungian community in Iceland, my journey through his writings was a solitary one. They held me captive and flung open doors to my inner recesses. At the time of the dream, I participated in a dream group in New York led by a Jungian analyst. It was a community unlike any I had belonged to. I fell in love with the dream work, which infused my life with excitement and magic. However, I kept this new-found interest hidden from family and friends in Iceland and from my fellow students at the university. Although many scholars had a burning interest in our folkloric past, it seemed clear to me that they considered themselves far removed from the "superstition" that inspired this heritage and was to be attributed to the ancestors' inability to differentiate between imagination and reality. Or so I understood. If at the outset, my secrecy was induced by the fear of being ridiculed for taking my dreams seriously, the truth is that I had myself been prejudiced towards those around me who did so. It seemed that their approach to the dreamlife was pretty superficial as if it had nothing to do with the subjective self. I now found myself pitted against my own prejudice and felt that I needed to justify my interest in my nocturnal adventures with sensible arguments about inner work. I experienced profound insecurity in the face of a reality that did not lend itself to academic reasoning. At the same time I was held back by the sense of the sacred that attaches to the dream and makes it both delicate and intimately personal. I had been introduced to a world so different from the one I had hitherto shared with my community of friends that I did not know how to give voice to it. The fear of making a fool of myself had been a lifelong companion that shut *me* up within myself. I now knew that I had to break free. But before I could begin to share my experiences outside the circle of fellow dreamers, I needed to find attunement to *my* music. I believe it was in response to that fundamental need that my unconscious sent me the dream about the poet and the silver necklace.

One could ask what would have happened if I had not responded to this silent voice that spoke to me from my depths. I would have kept the hiding game going and been miserable for betraying a vital part of myself. From Jung, I have learned that when we are dominated by an imbalance of this sort, the unconscious tries to redress the balance. If it does not succeed in leading us on the right track by gentle means, it may try to shake us up by the intrusion of a nightmare like—say—the 13th wise woman in "Thorn-Rose" (Chapter 3). In its silent voice, it screams: "Now you must change your ways!" Which begs the question: Has the 13th wise woman reached our ears as a collective? Could it be that the unbalanced state of affairs in our world is due to the fact that we have not yet grasped her message? With the war waged on menstruation today, it looks like we are following in the footsteps of the fairy tale king and still await Thorn-Rose's awakening to a more mature reality.

The name of the poet whom my dream had presented to me as the giver of unexpected treasures is Thor*steinn* from *Hamar*. *Steinn* means "stone" and *Hamar*, the name of the farm where the poet grew up and with which he associates himself, means "cliff." These names suggested to me that my dreaming self had forged a link between my dream-necklace and that of the goddess who acquired hers from dwarfs who lived in a stone. To drive the message home, my name *Hall-fríður* is a compound the meaning of which is "stone" and "she who is loved." The dream not only lent a new dimension to my name, inherited from my maternal grandmother who bestowed unconditional love on me and whom I have come to see as the "fairy godmother" of my childhood, it also took me to deep and unknown places in myself. The genius of the dream-maker defies comprehension. By name, I am "she who is loved in the stone." The challenge put to me by the dream was to find her in me.

While digging fervently into this dream symbol, I engaged in deep dialogue with my dreaming self, which led to pendants and necklaces surfacing galore in my dreams. Jung defined a symbolic image that moves the dreamer in this way as the best possible expression of a psychic content of which the dreamer is unconscious or not fully conscious but which she or he needs to integrate in order to evolve and fulfill her or his potential. In order to get the message across, the unconscious keeps hammering on it, in different guises if need be, until the dreamer grasps its meaning and integrates it into her way of being in the world. Understanding by itself does not suffice; the individual has to act in accordance with the new understanding. We see repetitions of this kind in fairy tales and folk tales. Often three attempts are needed before the hero attains the treasure, whereby the problem that set the quest in motion is resolved. In "The Outcast," for example, it is the third sister who brings back the fire and lights the way to redemption for a community shackled by materialism and greed (Chapter 9).

In the previous chapter I explained how I came to understand that, as a character in my dream, Thorsteinn from Hamar personified a latent desire in me to connect with and bring out the poet in myself. It could be argued that I had an intimate spiritual relationship with him through his poems by which I was moved and to which I made a deep connection. By the same token, I understood that Freyja's intercourse with the dwarfs was of a spiritual nature and her jewel a promise engendered by that spiritual union. The dwarfs are master smiths who mediate images from the creative wellspring to the conscious mind. And so do poems, forged in the smithy of a poet who lends voice to unfathomable truths that expand our horizons.

Freyja stayed four nights in the stone. The number four is a universal symbol of wholeness, as can be inferred from the four phases of the moon, the four directions, the four seasons, and so on. The four dwarfs with whom Freyja slept call to mind the four dwarfs named after the cardinal directions who were said to hold up the sky. I imagine that the fact that the woman bleeds and comes healed out of her seclusion gave rise to the idea of healing inherent in wholeness, of being whole in oneself and being at one with the universe. Every creative person needs to be in relationship with his or her inner nature, and symbolism that induces creation reflects the intercourse of opposites in some form. The intercourse between a man and a woman begets a biological offspring, but the intercourse between the conscious personality and the collective unconscious engenders a new vision that can promote growth and evolution on an individual as well as on a collective level. Freyja's Brísingamen is an example of the latter. In essence, it teaches us to reach for the unity beyond opposites, to heal the split between spirit and matter.

As previously explained, the word *Brísingamen* is a compound noun, the first half of which refers to "flames of fire" while the latter part is identical with the "moon" root *men*. Jungian analyst Erich Neumann demonstrates how etymology has attempted to separate the "moon"-root *men* and the "spirit"-root *manas* while, in actuality, they derive from the same Sanskrit root *mati-h*, which on the one hand means "thought, intension [sic]" and "measure, knowing" on the other. "The single archetypal root underlying" the various meanings that have branched out from this source "is the moon-spirit."[1] This fundamental unity I see reflected in Freyja's Brísingamen as described before:

> Freyja's adventure conjures up an image of the descending sun who abandons herself in the dissolving embrace of the moon in its dark phase, her red embers bleeding from under his coal-black disk, arranged in a flaming necklace.[2]

As *men* means "pendant, necklace" in Icelandic, the natural phenomenon in which Brísingamen is seemingly rooted has been overlooked. That this celestial display still exerts a powerful attraction on modern man is borne out by this poetic description:

> Nothing quite matches the experience of viewing a total eclipse of the Sun. Whether it's the coal-black disk of the Moon set against the ghostly, pearly white corona, the solar prominences arranged like a necklace of rubies around the lunar limb, or the spectacular diamond ring bursting forth from behind a deep lunar valley, the image of an eclipse will remain forever etched in a viewer's mind.[3]

---

1   1954, pp. 84-85.

2   From my text about Freyja (as per note 1).

3   Edwin L. Aguirre. "Imaging a Solar Eclipse". Obtained on Jan. 11, 2003 from http://www.skyandtelescope.com/article_99_1.asp.

There are those who project the eye of God onto the solar eclipse. For the poets of old, Freyja's tears were a metaphor for gold, and one can speculate whether it was this celestial image that gave rise to the identification of Freyja's tear with *red-gold*:

> Od went far away, but Freyja stays behind and cries, but her tear is *red-gold*.[4]

In her book, *The Cassandra Complex: Living with Disbelief*, Laurie Schapira refers to the truth-seeing third eye as "the dark vaginal eye of the goddess."[5] This is the eye that looks within. From this point of view, it is tempting to read the above quote as a euphemistic description of menstrual bleeding. Freyja was a *völva*. It is a denomination that refers to her role as a "seeress" and points to the womb as the source of divine wisdom (cf. Lat. *volva, vulva* ="womb"), as does the name Delphi given to the seat of the famous oracle (from Gr. *delphus, delphys* = "womb"). In *The Wise Wound: The Myths, Realities, and Meanings of Menstruation*, Penelope Shuttle and Peter Redgrove point out that the single eye as an emblem of the goddess was widespread in ancient cultures, and they suggest that it may have originated from the "single-eye appearance of the inner vagina."[6] The womb is a mysterious place of life-giving and death-dealing. This ambivalent meaning was seemingly transferred on to the goddess's eye as we will see hinted at in "The 'Hidden Woman' in Hafnanúpur" (Chapter 4).

Brísingamen was Freyja's attribute and would have emphasized her role as a *völva*. The merging of the opposites suggested by its

---

4   Snorri Sturluson. "Gylfaginning," ch. 35; italics mine.

5   P. 111. Cassandra was a Troyan princess, on whom the god Apollo bestowed the gift of prophecy in exchange for sexual favors. When she refused to fulfill her part of the bargain after accepting his gift, he put on her the curse that nobody would believe her prophecies.

6   Shuttle and Redgrove, pp. 179-180; they so describe the birth-cone of the womb in its place of entry at the top of the vaginal passage, as seen through a speculum: "One sees a cone, with the tip missing, and an aperture, like the pupil of an eye" (p. 179).

name would have been the key to achieving the ecstacy or trance, which was a prerequisite for transmitting information from the unconscious. And as the seat of vocal expression, the neck is a gate through which divine wisdom exits into the world. The ritual that aimed at achieving the altered state of consciousness symbolized by Brísingamen was called *seiðr* and, according to the scant information that exists, it involved the singing of spells. This art was taught to Odin and his pantheon by Freyja.

The *völva* was thus a prophetess, a sibyl, who mediated her visions to the community. *Völuspá* ("The Prophecy of the Seeress") is an Eddic poem that dates back to the 10th century, the time at which Christianization was taking place in the Nordic countries. The *völva* claims silence of all who listen, but her prophecy is addressed primarily to Odin. She begins by reciting her memory of the time before his reign and ends with her vision of the end of his corrupt world as the flaming earth sinks into the sea, and fire consumes the heaven. But she also foresees that the earth, fresh and green, will rise anew out of the ocean. Here Odin presents the *völva* with a necklace (*men*) and rings in exchange for her prophecy. It is as if the ring motif, the circle, emphasizes the cycles of life reflected in the poem itself. As one cycle ends, a new cycle, built on the experience garnered from the previous one, begins. And nowhere is cyclicity more visible than in the moon (*men*) and its partner, the *men*struating female.[7]

As a fertility goddess, Freyja personified the Sun (*Sól*), and in ancient poetic language the Moon (*Máni*) is presented as a personage belonging to the race of giants.[8] *Thurs* (Ice. þurs) is a pejorative denomination for giant. "You look like a *thurs*," says the god Thor to the dwarf *Alvís* ("the omniscient"), who has come to claim the

---

7   Shuttle and Redgrove point out that the Greek Sybils prophesied once a month and conclude that "one cannot believe that their shamanism was unrelated to their menstrual periods, particularly as their own statements speak of possession by lunar spirits" (p. 147).

8   Simek, p. 166.

god's daughter as his bride.[9] Here, Thor uses a word associated with giants to describe his impression of the unwelcome dwarf. The encounter between the god and the dwarf reads like a comic allusion to Freyja's bridal episode in the stone which apparently was a thorn in the god's side, for in another poem he prides himself of having gone east and "battered giants / evil brides, / who went to the rock."[10]

Thurs is also the name attributed to the Þ-rune which corresponds to the letter þ, called "thorn" (Ice. þorn). A Norwegian rune poem from the 12th century explains that "*thurs* causes the sickness of women" and an Icelandic poem from the 15th century states that "*thurs* is the torment of women / and an inhabitant of rocks." Indications are that *thurs* was intimately linked with menstruation. The dwarf's intrusion into the halls of Thor and his claim on the god's daughter suggests that no more than the king, Thorn-Rose's father, did the gods have the power to oust and isolate themselves from menstrual nature. The poem shows Thor outsmarting the *omniscient* dwarf by detaining him until the sun came up, at which point he turned to stone. I would not be surprised if this is the very stone that the alchemists searched for in their laboratories!

The rune poems show that the oppressor's aggressive hammering against the female's intimate communion with her lunar other had had its intended effect. What before was conceived of as a precious gift in the broadest sense of the word, had by now become a suffering caused by evil. The oppressor had planted himself in the female psyche... How do I convey the revelation that strikes me like lightning as I am writing this?! All of a sudden the gift from my dream poet appears in a new light. I know this has been brewing in me, but it is only now that the message breaks through, loud and clear. The poet's name is a compound: *Thor-steinn*. He is thus the

---

9   *Alvíssmál* ("Lay of Alvís"), st. 2.

10   *Hárbarðsljóð*, ("Lay of Harbard"), st. 23.

namesake of Thor and associated with "stone." My dream poet's gift, it turns out, is the oppressor's offer of reconciliation, an attempt to bring about a union between contending parts of myself. One has to wonder how the dreaming mind comes up with such ingenious symbolism in its attempt to reach the conscious personality and solicit its cooperation in breaking free of an age-old indoctrination.

Little by little clues fall into place. Thor's weapon was a hammer, and the poet associates himself with his native farm, *Hamar* ("hammer"). Thor wielded his hammer unsparingly on the giants' head, smashing their skull to pieces. Finally, the slice of *pound* cake, on top of which my dream poet put a silver key ring, makes sense to me. The dream maker, I have come to know, has a delightful sense of humor! Thor was a thundergod. His hammer, based on the idea of lightning, is a murderous weapon in the myths. The poet's approach in my dream was of an entirely different nature, generous and loving. In both cases, transformation is the intended effect. The god's hammer pounding on a giant's head no doubt symbolized the breaking up of petrified thought patterns. By the same token, Thorsteinn's poems had planted a transformative seed in me by turning my gaze toward "the silent, hidden, archaic, behind all that is," whereby an unravelling of my learned prejudgements was set in motion.

At the beginning of this chapter, I touched on the elevated description of Thorunn's personality in "The 'Hidden Woman' in Hafnanúpur" and the powerful influence such stereotypes effectuate. An ode to Freyja has been dedicated as a toast to Icelandic women, implying that each of us, old and young, incarnates the goddess. On festive occasions, the male population rises in our honor and sings with inspired vigor (in my loose translation):

> You Freyja of the fosterland,
> you beautiful Goddess of the Vanir,
> mother, wife, and maiden,
> accept our acclaim and praise.

Blessed be your gentle
smile and golden tear.
You've shone on our land and folk
your light for a thousand years.
                    Matthias Jochumsson (1835-1920)

This eulogy to a gently smiling goddess who cries golden tears, composed by a Christian minister one thousand years after the settlement in 874 of the Norse Vikings in Iceland, is in odd contrast to the coarse denunciation of Freyja as "a bitch" by one of the proponents of Christianity at the Icelandic Althing in 999:

> "I do not wish to vilify the gods,
>   but I think Freyja is a bitch."

It seems fair to assume that since the time of Christianization the goddess has been softened and domesticated to better serve as inspiration for women to fulfill the roles paid homage to in the poem. The important question is whether this development has taken place on women's own terms.

In the rare glimpses we catch of Freyja in the myths, she is by no means always gentle and smiling. In *Þrymskviða* ("Lay of Thrym") the fuming goddess bears a closer resemblance to the farmer's daughter turned giantess in the folktale "The Farmer at Fossvellir" (Chapter 7) than the description of the nineteenth century minister. She swells with anger so that Brísingamen bursts open at Thor's suggestion that she accompany him to the giant world to retrieve his stolen hammer. Her fury is that of a giantess as she causes the hall of the gods to quake and quiver. Thrym, the lord of *thurses*, has claimed her as his bride in return for the stolen good. While the poem is an allusion to Freyja's bridal episode in the stone and her alliance with the fertility cult of the Vanir—in fact one of her cognomens is "Bride of the Vanir," it emphasizes Freyja's sovereignty over herself. We saw this already in the description of her dominion over her bower. She does not let herself be ordered around, one way or the other. In this she is the opposite of the farmer's daughter in the tale who is the victim of both feminine nature and God's representative on earth, a minister who shuts her up in a cave in the company of four giants. We recognize the theme. The folk tale shows that not only did man fear outer nature, as is revealed by annals from the period when the events it describes were supposed to have taken place, but also the menstrual nature of woman, which he has restrained and controlled with questionable means and ridicule.

We can react to suppression with furious anger like the farmer's daughter in the tale or subject ourselves to it with detrimental consequences for our body and soul like Thorunn in "The 'Hidden Woman' in Hafnanúpur." What we desire is to be ourselves, to find our own rhythm, and flower on our own terms. In order to achieve this, we need to find our way back to our roots, and we need to be aware that we are not only dealing with cultural stereotypes but also with forces in our psyches that our gods and goddesses have come to personify. If every woman carries Freyja within like our minister poet asserts, we need to understand what Freyja represents so that we know how to channel that energy in a conscious and constructive manner. Of course Freyja is present in men too, and the problem we women come up against is that the image we get of her in the myths, and in the above poem, is presented from the viewpoint of Christian males. She was slandered as a bitch by the lawmaker and Christian missionary at the juncture of heathendom and Christianity and was praised as a gentle creature who smiles through golden tears by a Christian minister nine centuries later. Is it any wonder that we ask: who was Freyja? At this time when alienation reigns rampant, I believe that it is of vital importance that we reconnect to the goddess of love and fertility. What follows is a quest for such a reunion.

3
Thorn-Rose

from Steingrímur Thorsteinsson's
Book of Fairy Tales

Once upon a time, there was a king and a queen. Every day they said: "If only we had a child!" But their prayer was not answered. Then one day, when the queen was bathing, a crab crawled on land from the water's edge and said: "Your wish will be fulfilled and you will have a daughter."

The crab's prophecy came true, and the queen gave birth to a girl child so beautiful that the king was beside himself with joy and called for a public celebration. Not only did he invite relatives and friends to the festivities but also wise women, so that they would all be loyal and well-disposed toward the child. There were thirteen of those in his kingdom, but as he owned only twelve gold plates to serve them on, he could not invite the thirteenth. Now those who were invited arrived, and as the feast came to an end, they bestowed their miraculous gifts on the child. One gave her chastity, another beauty, the third wealth, and thus one after the other they gave to the child everything that was of greatest value in the world. But when eleven had pronounced their wishes, the thirteenth, who had not been invited, came with the intention of avenging herself. She called out and said: "In her fifteenth year, the princess shall prick herself on a spindle and drop dead."

Then the twelfth, who had not yet pronounced her wish, stepped forth; she could not erase the evil doom, but temper it she could, and so she said: "Yet the princess shall not die but lie asleep for a hundred years."

The king, hoping that he would nonetheless be able to protect his child from this evil prediction, ordered that all the spindles in the kingdom be destroyed. But everything the wise women had said manifested in the princess, for so beautiful, virtuous, kind and wise was she, that everyone who laid eyes on her was bound to love her dearly.

Then it happened one day that the king and the queen were away from home but their daughter, who was fully fifteen at the time, was left by herself in the palace. She walked about hither and thither as she pleased, exploring parlors and rooms. Finally she came to an old tower. She ascended a narrow staircase and came upon a small door. There was a gold key in the lock. She turned the key and the door swung open. She then came into a small room where an old woman busied herself with spinning flax. "What are you doing here, mother dear!" says the princess. – "I am spinning flax," replies the old woman nodding her head. – "How gaily that thing twirls around!" said the princess, and she seized the spindle and intended to start spinning. But no sooner had she touched the spindle than the wise woman's prophecy came true, and she pricked her finger.[1]

She immediately fell to the ground, and heavy sleep came over her. The king and the queen now came home, and they too fell asleep, along with the entire court. The horses fell asleep in the stable and the dogs in the garden, the pigeons on the roof and the flies on the wall. The fire that burned in the hearth slowed down and fell asleep; the sizzling frying-sound fell silent and the meat stopped cooking; the cook was about to tear the kitchen boy's hair out for he had made some mistake, but that came to naught. He let go of him and fell asleep. Thus sleep and dead silence spread over everything that lived and breathed.

A thornhedge then began to grow around the palace, and it continued to grow from one year to the next, till it reached around and above it, so nothing was to be seen of it, not even the weathercocks on the roof. But all over the country, people told the tale of the beautiful, sleeping Thorn-Rose, for that was what the princess was called, and from time to time princes ventured to break through the hedge to get into the palace. But it was an endeavor doomed to fail, for the thorns were like claws that grabbed each other. The princes became stuck between them and suffered a pitiful death.

Now many, many years went by and a certain prince passed through the country. An old man told him about the thornhedge and mentioned that people believed there was a palace behind it, and asleep in this palace was a beautiful princess whose name was Thorn-Rose, and along with her the entire court. He also told him, as he himself had been told by his grandfather, that the princes who had tried to break through the thornhedge had become stuck in it and suffered a torturous death.

---

1   Literally in Thorsteinsson's rendition: *and she pricked herself on the rod.* In *Dornröschen*, from which his translation is made, it is specified that the princess pricks her finger: "Kaum hatte sie die Spindel angerührt, so ging der Zauberspruch in Erfüllung, und sie stach sich damit in den Finger" (http://www.grimmstories.com/de/grimm_maerchen/dornroschen). As I believe that this is a significant detail, I have opted to follow the original version.

"This will not deter me," said the young prince, "I am going to break through the hedge and see the beautiful Thorn-Rose." The old man tried in every way to discourage him, but it was to no avail.

But now it so happened that on the day the prince arrived the one hundred years had passed. When he came to the thornhedge, it had turned into big and beautiful flowers which disentangled by themselves so that he passed through safe and sound, but everything closed again on his heels and became a hedge as before. He now came into the palace. Horses and speckled deerhounds slept in the palace garden but on the roof sat pigeons with their heads stuck under their wings. As he came in, he saw the flies asleep on the walls. The cook in the kitchen had his hand still aloft, the kitchen maid was in the midst of plucking a black hen. The prince walked further in and came upon the people of the court sleeping in a heap and the king with his queen on top. He went further still and finally came to the tower and opened the door to the little room in which Thorn-Rose was sleeping.

She lay there and was so lovely that he could not take his eyes off her, and he bent over her and kissed her. But when he had given her the kiss, she opened her eyes, awakened from her sleep and smiled to him. They now went down together, and the king and the queen along with all the people of the court woke up and looked at each other in wonder. The horses in the garden stood up and shook themselves, the deerhounds engaged in play and wiggled their tails, and the pigeons pulled their heads from under their wings and flew into the fields. The flies started to crawl on the wall, the fire came alive and blazing in the kitchen so the food got cooked and the roast crackled; the cook smacked the kitchen boy so that he screamed and the kitchen maid finished plucking the hen. The prince now *drank his wedding*[2] to Thorn-Rose and they lived happily together for the rest of their lives.

---

2   This archaic expression has its roots in a Celtic ritual in which a new king wed himself to the goddess of the land, Lady Sovereignty, by drinking from a cup offered him by her mortal representative. Thorn-Rose is thus an incarnation of the goddess from whom the prince accepts his rulership as a new king who brings a new order to the collective. Icelandic writer Svava Jakobsdottir has illustrated this sacred custom in her novel *Gunnlaðar saga* ("Saga of Gunnlöd"), a work inspired by Odin's legendary theft of the mead of poetry from Gunnlöd, who was its guardian.

INTERPRETATION

Shroud of Silence

Menstruation has long been veiled by a mysterious silence in our culture. In fairy tales, myths, and folk tales this intimate female reality is concealed in symbols and metaphors. As previously mentioned, "The Witch's Ride" is the only tale in the six volumes of *Icelandic Folk and Fairy Tales* that deals with menstrual blood in plain terms. While this provoking tale presents the blood as sustenance for the Devil, it allows us to glimpse the "mead of poetry" through its thinly disguised plot. Because of the secrecy surrounding menstrual blood in our lives and culture, scholars who dedicated themselves to making our heritage accessible to us, and who for the most part were males, overlooked this important part of female experience in their interpretation of these old stories.

A better know title for the tale of Thorn-Rose is "Sleeping Beauty." One afternoon a long time ago, I happened on a radio program about the child psychologist Bruno Bettelheim and his ideas concerning the therapeutic value of fairy tales for kids. This was the first time I heard this familiar tale associated with menstruation.[3] Although I don't recall the details of the presentation, the moment is still

---

3   Picking up his book, *The Uses of Enchantmen: The Meaning and Importance of Fairy Tales,* after having finished my text, I find that as far as menstruation is concerned his analysis rhymes with my impressions. He states that "in times past, fifteen was often the age at which menstruation began," and he associates the thirteen fairies with the thirteen lunar months. "Thus," he says, "the number of twelve good fairies plus a thirteenth evil one indicates symbolically that the fatal 'curse' refers to menstruation." He traces the use of the word "curse" for menstruation to the Bible, where it is said to be "inherited by woman from woman." That, he explains, is why the bleeding in the tale comes about through an encounter with "an old woman, not a man" (pp. 232-233). He puts forth the wonderful observation that "the king, the male, does not understand the necessity of menstruation and tries to prevent his daughter from experiencing the fatal bleeding," while "the queen, in all versions of the story, seems unconcerned with the prediction of the angry fairy. In any case she knows better than to try to prevent it."

very much alive in my memory—my surroundings, the time of day, the presenter's voice. In retrospect, I believe that this was a more meaningful chance encounter than I realized at the time. When the menstrual meaning concealed in Freyja's Brísingamen was sprung open for me[4], my interest in exploring this hidden theme in my heritage was awakened. This was when that moment from long ago came back to me. Thorn-Rose is the one tale in this collection that cannot be defined as Icelandic. Its roots, however, reach deep into the soil of the Icelandic people's Germanic ancestry and hence it forms an enlightening backdrop for the tales that follow.

Today, the interpretation of "Thorn-Rose" as a tale of initiation is no longer a novelty. The dramatic event takes place when Thorn-Rose is fifteen. Considering that the average age at menarche in the West today is twelve to thirteen years, we might think this an invalid interpretation. It is said, however, to be well-documented that from 1850 to 1960 there was a decline in age from seventeen to thirteen in Europe.[5] Statistics also show that in present times menstruation begins at a later age in females from less developed countries.[6] The tale of Thorn-Rose is of European origin and from a timeless past.

"Aunt Rosa is on visit" was a euphemism used by us girls when we were having our period. Where did this benevolent metaphor come from? I wonder whether we did not sense, deep down, that we had a *spinster* relative within whose desire it was to guide us toward the spiritual-creative source inherent in the dissolving phase of the flow. In my interpretation, I will attempt to unwrap the *gift*[7] of the 13th Wise Woman and explore its meaning for women. As paradoxical

---

4   In Icelandic the word *men* as a pendant or a necklace, is often used for a locket. A locket frequently contains a secret that is close to the wearer's heart, such as photographs of lover and self. It struck me as an appropriate meaning for Freyja's jewel which I see as an emblem of the union of opposites.

5   http://en.wikipedia.org/wiki/Menarche.

6   http://pediatrics.aappublications.org/content/118/5/2245.full.

7   This is a reference to Annette Høst's interpretation of Sleeping Beauty "The Gifts of the 13th Fairy" in *Blessed by the Moon*. http://www.shamanism.dk/

as it may seem, the story suggests that it is something precious. Gift is the same as talent. We do not see Thorn-Rose make use of the talents menstruation bestows on woman; rather, are we likely to see her primarily as a lovely young girl whom many men desire and a courageous prince finally releases from an evil spell. At first sight, it might seem that the tale confirms the traditional gender roles that no longer fit our modern life style. But if we approach the story on a deeper level, we come to realize that there is more to this familiar tale than meets the eye.

Archetype of Female Initiation

Fairy tales are not anchored in a definite time or place: "Once upon a time there was a king and queen..." This is how the story of Thorn-Rose begins. Their plot takes place in timeless eternity and reveals dramatic events in the human psyche at the time of their emergence on the communal stage. Although those stories have roots in an archaic past, they reflect to us the same fundamental problems that we are dealing with today. On the surface, they seem infinitely distant from our familiar reality, but they have been shown to contain the purest presentation of the human psyche's fundamental patterns. They are a mirror in which we can see our very soul. Thorn-Rose represents the biological and psychological reality of all young women. She is an *archetype* as Carl Jung called those fundamental patterns shared by humanity. Every young girl goes through initiation into womanhood at the time of her first bleeding. However, it depends on the cultural code of her environment to determine how she experiences the profound changes that take place in her at this juncture in her life.

In many traditional societies, female initiation is channeled through certain rituals. In the Protestant culture I grew up in, it is the confirmation at age thirteen to fourteen that marks a young person's entry into the community of adults. But the confirmation ritual has no direct bearing on the physical and psychological changes a young girl is undergoing at this time. It is not the newly discovered blood trickling from her body that is being celebrated at the altar, but that of the male Christ, which He shed on the cross for our sins as corporeal beings. Although the onset of menstruation is increasingly regarded as an occasion for celebration in our fast-paced, materialist culture, young women may not be fully aware of its power and spiritual dimension. The story of Thorn-Rose may help shed light on this.

Messenger from the Deep Blue Sea

As is true of every fairy tale, there is something missing at the beginning. The royal couple cannot conceive. This means that the collective is stagnated and needs new blood to evolve. It is a crab that sets evolution in motion. Following in the footsteps of Carl Jung, psychologist Sibylle Birkhäuser-Oeri holds that images and motifs in fairy tales conceal a meaning not immediately obvious. Mining those tales for meaning can help us reconnect to the primitive who is still alive within us but with whom many of us have lost contact. Birkhäuser-Oeri stresses that this is no mere inferior part of our psyche but a source of vitality and creativity from which we have been cut.

Menstruation is a bond that links us through countless cycles to this primitive source. And given our premise, it is the evolutionary force in this tale that leads the collective out of a rut toward the resolution of a fundamental dilemma. Birkhäuser-Oeri explains that "partly what we hear in those tales is the voice of a very primitive mentality from a time when everything in the psyche was projected onto nature. Trees and animals had voices and expressed humanity's own unconscious thoughts and feelings."[8] From this point of view, the talking crab personifies the prophetic gift of the

8   P. 11.

queen which comes from a mysterious source outside the sphere of her conscious mind. Birkhäuser-Oeri emphasizes that "a fairy tale is an unconscious product of the imagination, just like a dream."[9] Marie-Louise von Franz, who was one of Jung's foremost disciples, believes that most frequently those tales originated in an individual encounter with the unconscious and then reached their present form through repetition and amplification as they spread from mouth to mouth.[10] From this perspective a fairy tale is a collective dream that refers to problems of a universal character.

It is not uncommon that animals visit us in dreams. An example is the snake in the dream of the 13-year-old American girl presented in the "Prelude." In my experience, we get a sense of the message animals carry even if it is not put into words. If, as an example, we dream of a dog we would reflect on the specific characteristics of that animal, like for instance its keen sense of smell and hearing, its instinctive ability to find its way which has led to its widespread symbolic role as a guide to the other world. From our interaction with the animal in the dream, and the feelings associated with it, we can infer how we relate to this nature in ourselves. Dreams have the practical function of alerting us to something of which we are not consciously aware and would be better off knowing.

As a domesticated animal the dog has a close relationship with man who is its undisputed master. A crab on the other hand is a cold blooded sea creature and stands for something that is alien to human consciousness. Yet it is part of the queen's psyche. Encased in its shell it points to an inscrutable mystery. This theme is echoed in the locked little room in the tower where Thorn-Rose encounters the spinster. The gold key that allows her to enter the room implies that she is being initiated into a mystery. The theme is again repeated in the thornhedge that rises and encloses Thorn-Rose, who has

9   P. 9.

10   1996, p. 24.

become part of the mystery and a "treasure hard to attain" whom princes desire and risk their lives for.

The crab is a primitive sea creature, and the sea, science tells us, was the cradle of life. As a symbol, the crab points to our origin, to our very roots, which we need to be connected to in order to evolve and fulfill our potential. The prophesying crab emerges from the depths and announces to the queen that she will give birth to a daughter. We are reminded of the celestial messenger Gabriel who announced to Mary that she would give birth to a son.

The Divine Daughter

We mentioned before that it is a lack that sets the story in motion. Thorn-Rose is one of the tales collected by the brothers Grimm. Marie-Louise von Franz traces the growing interest in fairy tales among German thinkers and writers in the eighteenth century to dissatisfaction with Christian teaching and a longing for a more vital, earthy, and instinctual wisdom. In her words: "It was this religious search for something which seemed lacking in official Christian teaching that first induced the famous brothers Jakob and Wilhelm Grimm to collect folktales."[11] If we look at our tale in this light, we realize that what is lacking in Christian teaching is the divine mother-daughter pair, represented here by the spinster and Thorn-Rose who addresses the old woman as "mother." The queen is Thorn-Rose's earthly mother, but the spinster, she who spins the thread of life, is Eternity incarnated. And significantly, she is spinning flax.

One of the names attributed to Freyja is *Hörn*, derived from *hör* which means "flax". This betrays a connection between Freyja and the spinster. In Chapter I we saw that leading up to the Christianization

---

11   Ibid., p. 4.

of Icelanders in the year 1000, the goddess and feminine face of Love was publicly decried as a "bitch" by a renowned lawmaker and Christian missionary. It is testimony to Freyja's important stature that the blasphemer was subjected to three years of exile. With the advent of Christianity, love poetry, said to be favored by Freyja, became forbidden by law, and a man who serenaded a woman risked a lifelong expulsion from human society. To the proponents of the new religion, the submissive Mary would have been a preferable model for womenfolk than was the unruly and independent goddess. Also, if we take a close look, does not Thorn-Rose's high-flown character description bear semblance to that attributed to the saintly Virgin?

As mentioned before, Freyja had a daughter called *Hnoss* ("treasure") by her husband Od, a wild spirit hidden from view in the myths and of whom we know nothing but the name which means "poem, poetry." In like manner, the daughter *Hnoss* is but a name that stands for something precious and sought after. And now we are getting close to Thorn-Rose who represents "the treasure hard to get" that princes seek and for whom they risk their lives. The spinster and the young heroine in the fairy tale seemingly embody the same archetypes as the goddess Freyja and her daughter Hnoss. And it is easy to imagine that the 13th Wise Woman incarnates the goddess' ire for having been exiled in our culture.

Etymology betrays an intimate relationship between the moon[12] and menstruation. In Chapter 1 we saw that the moon is masculine in Germanic languages. We also saw that "once upon a time" it was widely believed, and still is in some traditional societies, that menstruation was caused by the moon in the guise of a male, or a "dream husband," who had sexual intercourse with the woman at her period.[13] Hence first bleeding would be referred to as a deflowering. This tradition would explain Freyja's "hidden" husband and father

12 Derived from IE. *mēn-* = "month, moon," whence Lat. *mensis*, Gr. *mēn*= "month" and *mēne*= "moon."

13 Shuttle and Redgrove, pp. 96-99.

of her precious daughter, i.e., herself cleansed, reborn and ever renewed through her female descendants emerging from their seclusion along with the crescent moon.

By gleaning shards of our ancestors' repressed religion from the treasure trove of fairy tales, we gain a more complete picture of our psychological heritage and an enhanced ability to differentiate between the genuine and the false in ourselves and the culture. When the new religion replaced the old one, elements of the latter that did not serve the new order were demonized and repressed. The tale of Thorn-Rose shows, however, that what was "once upon a time" lives on in our psyches. If it is a question of a vital link in our psychological make-up, the repressed reality turns into dis-ease. Repression absorbs energy and blocks creativity. Such was the state of affairs in the sterile kingdom at the outset.

The Hermaphroditic Rose

We must not overlook that Thorn-Rose pricks her finger, which bleeds. The finger is a phallic symbol. This implies that menstruation has a phallic connotation. The tower, with the locked little room where the "disaster" occurs, I take to be a more ambivalent reference to the female genitalia. "We do not know / ourselves," says Sharon Olds in her poem "Am and Am not" as she reflects on the otherness of her "cunt," a stranger who has a will of its own: "Central inside me this one I am and am not, [...] / like a snake's reticulated body, rings of muscle- / like the penis outside-in, its twin."[14] The authors of the Wise Wound suggest that "what is most like a phallus inside the woman is the cervix of the womb, particularly at menstruation, when it ejaculates blood."[15] The finger would then be a displacement

---

14   P. 87.

15   Shuttle and Redgrove, p. 102.

from the actual site of bleeding, that is, from Thorn-Rose's "hidden" or invisible inner phallus.

In the quotations above, the female genitalia take on the image of an ejaculating phallus on the one hand and that of a receiving vessel on the other. In this, woman's sexual make-up is akin to the hermaphroditic rose. This twofold nature accords with the observed difference in her sexual expression at the two poles of her sexual peaks, menstruation and ovulation.[16] In the latter instance she feels most "loving" and "receptive," while around the time of flow her feelings express themselves in an "impatient demand" for sex. Also it is a period filled with "extroverted activity and urgency." These findings led to the conclusion that the latter period of sexuality was more "masculine" in character.[17] Not quite the image we get of sweet Thorn-Rose. And certainly not an ideal for a compliant wife!

Critics of the study object that its conclusions are laden with value judgements as the response at the time of ovulation is interpreted as "the highest form of female sexual expression," while the high point of sexual feeling around the time of flow is considered "an expression of a lesser (lower) form of sexuality."[18] The flaws in this study show how easily we fall prey to the received ideas of our culture when we really should be listening to our feelings and impulses and ask what they want from us.

Among the many studies on women's sexuality quoted by Shuttle and Redgrove are the writings of Havelock Ellis who considered the time of menstruation "an important time for erotic experience,

---

16   The study referred to was done in the 1930s by T. Benedek, psychoanalyst of Freudian persuasion, and B.B. Rubenstein, a clinician.

17   Weideger, pp. 121ff; Shuttle, pp. 84ff.

18   Ibid.

particularly imaginative auto-erotic experience and erotic dreams."[19] They add that he "regards the blood as a love-juice that flows with excitement." They also report a finding by Money and Ehrhardt[20], which reveals that as opposed to the desire to "surrender" felt at the time of ovulation, a desire to "capture and envelop" is more likely to be experienced around the menstrual period. This implies that the woman is more likely to take the erotic initiative and that, they suggest, could be threatening to a man.[21]

The desire to capture and envelop intimates that the opposite poles of aggressive (phallic) and receptive energies are aroused in woman at the time of the flow. If she cannot conceive and if nature is only concerned with propagating the species, why, one wonders, would she be sexually aroused? Might not nature have intended that her sexual impulse at this time be channeled in the service of evolution? Would not this be her fertile moment of spiritual conception, of the sacred marriage within, the seeds of which lead to her blossoming as a complete and creative individual? But as the menstrual pole of a woman's nature became demonized and repressed in the dominating culture, many women are at war with themselves during their period, without really knowing why. They have come to accept the pains and tribulations accompanying their periods as the natural state of affairs. The ideal embodied by sweet Thorn-Rose that they strive to meet, constellates the murderous rebel in them, embodied by the 13th Wise Woman who has to be repressed.

---

19   Author of *Studies in the Psychology of Sex* (1935). NY, 1942. They also quote him as saying: "The time may come when we must even change the divisions of the year for women, leaving to man his week and giving to her the same number of Sabbaths per year, but in groups of four successive days per month. When woman asserts her true physiological rights she will begin here, and will glory in what, in an age of ignorance, man made her think to be her shame." He also gives "impressive accounts of a woman in whom menstrual tension and release of sexual desire were reflected in her dreaming in bold acts, such as plunging into dangerous waters fully clothed" (p, 85).

20   (1972. *Man and Woman, Boy and Girl*, p. 223.)

21   Pp. 85-86.

Moon as Foundation of Consciousness

But what about the crab? In astrology, the Moon rules the sign of Cancer. Those who are familiar with Tarot will recognize the Moon-card in the initial scene of Thorn-Rose (see image). In the sky we see the Moon within the Sun and on the earthly plane beneath a crustacean crawling out of the water. Something is stirring in the unconscious and evolution is set in motion, the tortuous path of which lies between the wild (wolf) and the tame (dog) and leads from the mineral forms of life, through lush green fields toward distant blue mountain-tops of spiritual attainment. The implication is that the awakening to consciousness was brought about by the moon and its influence on early humans. The Moon-card thus reflects a beginning, while at the same time reminding us that every new beginning contains the seed of death as is manifested in the moon's cycles. In the context of the tale of Thorn-Rose, I see her prince's appearance on the earthly stage as a culmination of the long and arduous journey depicted on the card. I see him as an incarnation of a new masculine principle under the auspices of the lunar spirit.

As pointed out to me by Rachel Pollack, the Moon-card is often seen as a "regressive retreat from human consciousness to the wild beast, as if we must first reclaim our deep animal nature before we can journey to humanity." This is a pattern that runs through the tales of this collection. A woman reclaims her deep animal nature when she embraces and humanizes her wild, i.e. uncivilized, menstrual flow. In this tale, the regressive pull is symbolized by the queen's bathing in the pool where she encounters the crab who reveals to us her gift as a prophetess. She is the medium, the *völva*, who receives and conveys the message. As *völva*, she is a channel for the unadulterated voice of nature.

THE MOON

Even if time is suspended in the fairy tale, death is not done away with. In fact, the crab is simultaneously the carrier of a life-giving message and a harbinger of death. In Icelandic the word used casually for cancer is *krabbi* which means "crab," and so a crab is a glyph for the zodiacal sign Cancer. Death is woven into the fabric of life. Accordingly, Thorn-Rose and the prince, whose marriage will inaugurate a new ruling principle in the individual or collective psyche—"they lived happily together for the rest of their lives"—are mortal beings. No ruling principle is everlasting proves to be the optimistic note struck by the tale. The old king will die, if only symbolically, in yielding his power to the prince. The greatest inhibitor on our evolutionary path is undoubtedly our fear of death. The 13th Wise Woman holds this fear up to us. What she is really saying is that the image of the ideal maiden has to die and the whole of female experience needs to be embraced. I take the prince's reverent attitude toward the menarcheal girl to be an attainment of this ideal.

The Vicious Cycle

It is when the queen is relaxing in her bath that her unconscious lunar nature gains access to her solar consciousness in the guise of the crab. Thorn-Rose's prolonged sleep suggests that the gestation period from the seeding of an alien idea until its integration by the conscious personality or the collective is a long one. The demonizing of the blood has alienated woman from the soil of her feminine nature. If she is cut off from her roots, her spiritual evolution is curtailed. She becomes stuck in a predictable pattern, a vicious cycle. This is also true of our culture which to a great extent controls our mindset. We see this invisible control manifest in the king's decision to exclude the 13th Wise Woman from the celebration of his daughter's nativity because he has only 12 gold plates. Would not we think that he could have come up with a creative solution to this problem if he were not ruled by an uncontested order from above? In a culture that does not value menstruation, a woman is likely to experience it as a curse. The King within her, will resist its power with all his might. The Lord's decree, spelled out to Eve in the Garden of Eden, that she should be victim of her feminine nature, will continue to work its magic. This vicious cycle is echoed in the thornhedge, which may reflect the nasty effect of woman's negative stance towards her period. By fighting it she is likely to be victimized by the premenstrual syndrome, irritated and irascible due to her wrestle with the vengeful 13th Wise Woman who represents menstrual power gone destructive.

The repeated attempts of the princes who tried to break through the wicked thornhedge is another aspect of the same vicious cycle. What was required was a new and radically different approach. The reverent attitude of the prince whose desire it is to *see* the menarcheal girl enables Thorn-Rose to open up to him like a beautiful flower and receive him with a smile. The emphasis on *seeing* rather than conquering and dominating implies respectful acceptance of the full range of feminine reality. There is nothing that needs to be hidden.

Love is essentially all-inclusive, whether it be self-love or love of another. Love is in principle the opposite of self-interest. We cannot love a part of a person and not the whole. If we hate a part of ourselves, we project that hatred onto the world outside. Menstruation and mortal nature are a part of our make-up, enemies from which we seek refuge in the Kingdom of Heaven. But exiling the enemy from our consciousness does not do away with the energy invested in the entity. This is the message the 13th Wise Woman brings home. We must acknowledge her power and find a way to channel it in a creative and constructive manner.

Friday the 13th

I have already mentioned Annette Høst's interpretation of Sleeping Beauty, "The Gifts of the 13th Fairy." Høst, who is a shaman as was

Freyja, exhorts women to welcome the wild, untamable power that comes uninvited every month, to tune into it and be receptive to Nature and her spirits in a conscious and cooperative manner. By so doing, the curse will be transformed into a blessing.[22]

As we saw before, Høst associates the 12 gold plates with the solar principle and the unlucky number 13 with the moon. The solar calendar that we live by has 12 months in the year while the lunar calendar of our agriculturist ancestors had 13 moons in a year, and so does an unimpregnated woman have 13 periods a year. The belief that Friday the 13th will bring us bad luck persists to this day. This would be the day the 13th Wise Woman brings disaster on us!

Friday derives its name from Freyja, just as the Romans named this weekday *dies Veneris* for the goddess Venus. It is telling of the dramatic shift from heathendom to Christianity that the day previously associated with Love in the Icelandic language, *frjá*dagur (the verb *frjá* means "to love"), was changed to *föstu*dagur, which refers to fasting and hence chastening of the flesh. The implication is that we should not love our body which was deemed an obstruction rather than a vehicle towards spiritual growth. It is hard to believe that it was a coincidence that Christ's crucifixion took place on a Friday, a day consecrated to the Goddess of Love.

The Fury of the 13th Wise Woman

Let us take a closer look at what might have triggered the fury of the 13th Wise Woman. Her exclusion from the table at Thorn-Rose's natal feast smacks of the exclusion of menstruating women from the communion table of the early Christian Church.[23] Considering that once upon a time menstrual blood was regarded as a source of divine

---

22   "Blessed by the Moon" at http://www.shamanism.dk.

23   Weideger, p. 89.

wisdom, fertility, and healing, her spite becomes understandable. The king, who represents patriarchy's stance, exemplifies the urgent attempt we see in numerous tales to save the female from her menstrual nature under the pretext of a noble deed, namely, to free her from the grip of death. First the king attempts to oust menstruation, whereby he would have deprived his daughter of her natural rights, and then to eradicate it altogether by having all the spindles in his kingdom destroyed, a measure somewhat reminiscent of the medieval witch hunt when wise women were burned at the stake by the masses.[24] But woman's menstrual cycle is subjected to the laws of nature and not to the will of man, even if he is a king. The war against the dangerous intruder is still going on though, and has now taken on the guise of a pill. The culture's negative attitude toward menstruation continues to make of women an easy prey for exploitation, this time by a gigantic pharmaceutical industry.

Running like a red thread through our myths and tales are examples of how the ruling powers have endeavored to tame feminine nature and subject it to their interests. But the thornhedge, which grows without restraint, reminiscent of a virgin forest, is testimony to the wildness of the menstrual power that does not yield to the relentless attempts of the heroic spirit to *win* the maiden and confine her to the role of a submissive wife. An example of just such a struggle is the subjugation of Brynhild who was encircled by a wall of flickering flame, an image I imagine was derived from the solar prominences whirling around the black lunar limb during an eclipse of the sun.

Brynhild was a Valkyrie. *Valkyrie* is "she who chooses the slain." The Valkyries were called Odin's "wish maidens." As such their role

---

24   Bruno Bettelheim points out that *distaff*, that is, the staff on which the flax, wool, etc. is wound for use in spinning, has come to stand for female in general (p, 232). A staff was an attribute of the *völva* or "wise woman" (see Chapter 6). Possibly that symbolism was associated with the distaff to emphasize the *völva's* descendency from the Norns.

was to carry out the war god's will on the battlefield and escort the slain to Valhalla. But Brynhild was unruly. She felled an old king to whom Odin had promised victory and gave victory to a young one. In revenge, Odin stung her with a sleeping thorn and decreed that she should never have victory in war again and that she should marry. She vowed in turn that she would not marry any man who yielded to fear. Did Brynhild's strong-mindedness evoke the cyclic replacing of the old moon by the new moon in the mind of Odin, himself an ancient moon god? It would seem that Odin got scared. So he bought himself time by laying a spell on her and putting her to sleep. In the end, though, fate caught up with him and his world collapsed.

The Valkyries were spiritual beings who could take on the shape of birds and were in particular associated with the swan and often referred to as "swan maidens." Swans are known for loyalty to their mate, c.f. this telling title of a recent Icelandic play, *Swans do not Divorce*. In one Eddic poem, *Helreið Brynhildar* ("Brynhild's Ride to Hel"), the Valkyrie declares that at the age of twelve she had pledged a vow to the young king, "brother of *Auda* ('Fortune')," to whom she gave victory.[25] Twelve is frequently an age of initiation. Suffices to mention Jesus' teaching in the temple at age twelve. This fleeting glimpse into Brynhild's past suggests that the Valkyries resisted to succumb to the solar hero's worldview and break their blood bond to the lunar deity.

Where did the Valkyries' power come from? One suspects from the womb that menstruates at the dark of the moon. For that reason, they were also associated with the raven, a bird of prophetic wisdom and a harbinger of death. As our ancestresses were likely to be pregnant or breast-feeding during most of their fertile years,

---

25 Sts. 6 & 8.

they would have menstruated rarely.[26] Might this have led to single women, the *spinsters*, becoming suspect because of their regular encounters with the dark powers? It is a documented fact that women who lived by themselves were the primary victims of the witch hunt in the middle ages. A *spinster* might thus have been someone who needed to be eliminated, if not by marriage then by death. Would not the king's decree that all the spindles in the kingdom should be destroyed imply as much? No spindle, no spinster.

Brynhild was awakened by Sigurd, the dragon slayer and "greatest hero of all times," but then the story gets complicated and the lovers become separated through betrayal and deceit. Brynhild's father, king Budli, reinforced Odin's decree and gave his daughter an ultimatum: either she would marry the man of his choice or she would be left destitute and without his friendship.[27] She succumbed and agreed to marry him who would ride through the fire encircling her abode. Sigurd performed the deed in the guise of her wooer and his friend, Gunnar, who failed the test. When Brynhild found out that she had been tricked into marrying a "false" hero, whereby she had broken her vow not to marry a man whom fear could conquer, her vengefulness left behind a trail of blood, leading to the death of all involved.

Gerd, a giant maiden, was also encircled by a wall of fire—and by a wooden fence to boot, with two ferocious dogs guarding the gate—when Skírnir, the emissary of Freyr, a fertility god and

---

26 In the Introduction to his book *Is Menstruation Obsolete?* (NY, 1999), Elsimar M. Coutinho says: "It is reasonable to assume that at the dawn of the human epoch women menstruated rarely or not at all - it would have been extraordinary for a woman to menstruate regularly" (p. 2). Apparently the advocates of menstrual suppression use the infrequency of menstruation among our prehistoric ancestresses as an argument for their claim that cyclic menstruation is not natural (Elizabeth Kissling. "Pills, Periods, and Postfeminism: The New Politics of Marketing Birth Control" on http://www.tandfonline.com/doi/full/10.1080/14680777.2012.712373#. UyS_7IWqRoV). Dr. Coutinho is a passionate advocate of menstrual suppression and hence a true descendant of the fairy tale king, Thorn-Rose's father. He considers his "greatest contribution to humanity: the theory that menstruation is harmful and superfluous." Obtained 1/15/15 on http://www.elsimarcoutinho.com/o-medico/?lang=en.

27 "Völsunga saga," ch. 29.

Freyja's twin, rode through the roaring flames and forced her to give herself in marriage to the god. We will look at that myth later in connection with "Katla's Dream" (Chapter 5). The tale of Thorn-Rose is seemingly inspired by the same motif as those myths but with a different twist. Unlike king Budli, Brynhild's father, the king in this tale does not seem to have a saying in the betrothal of his daughter. The union is brought about by the breaking of a spell. It is as if this tale contains the promise of healing and peace between feuding tendencies in the human psyche, which have colored the life on our planet from time immemorial.

The images of the impenetrable thornhedge and the circle of fire may be vestiges of menstrual seclusion practiced by Germanic women "once upon a time" and from which men, jealous of their wives' erotic affair with the wild and poetic moon spirit, were excluded. By excluding the 13th Wise Woman from Thorn-Rose's natal feast the king's gesture might be seen as an attempt to turn the tables. If before menstrual seclusion was initiated by the women themselves as many believe, then the king's measure may reflect its becoming enforced by the male dominated culture that feared its revolutionary power. Today, this primal fear often takes on the expression of ridicule and feigned commiseration induced by her impossible temper tantrums around the time of the flow.

Yet another metaphor of the same order as the thornhedge and the wall of fire, is the virulent serpent that bites its tail and girdles the virginal bower. The circle form echoes the menstrual cycle which reflects in a nutshell the cyclical death and rebirth of the moon and the seasons.

The Sleep

The duration of sleep in menstrual tales is generally three or four days, i.e., the length of the period, and points to the attraction the body exerts on the mind which is envisioned as sleeping. The implication is that woman's conscious personality is not in control during the period. At this time, she is pulled into her primal nature, which speaks to her in a language quite different from that of her culture where the validity of feelings and sensations tends to be put down. It speaks to her about wonders yet to be uncovered, of things repressed. In the absence of words to express that which lies outside the limits of the civilized mind, her inner self conveys its messages to her in images. She becomes a "seeress." What fairy tales teach us is that Nature cannot but speak Truth. And as nature speaks Truth, so do dreams. They tell us the truth about ourselves and about our world.

In Chapter 2 we talked about the *völvas* and the ritual of *seiðr* which aimed at achieving an altered state of consciousness in order to access the objective psyche. I imagine this would have amounted to putting the ego with its indoctrinated ideas to sleep. Maybe that is why practicing *seiðr* was considered shameful for men whose model of behavior was the ever vigilant hero. At the beginning of our tale, the queen is relaxing in a bath when the crab emerges spontaneously from the deep psyche with a message that sets in motion a process that, in my view, has not yet run its course. The queen is presented to us as a *völva*, but not outright. She is the one who receives and mediates the message, but her gift is projected on the crab and she recedes into the background. This already hints at the repression of the *völva* as a mouthpiece for the feminine side of god. That suspicion is borne out by the exclusion of the 13th Wise Woman whose prophecy runs counter to the king's interests. This is emphasized by dramatization. The king is stuck in the predictable pattern of his male-oriented culture, which aims for immortality and cannot come up with a creative solution to welcome the 13th Wise Woman, who nonetheless turns out to be a necessary force in bringing about transformation in his sterile kingdom. For a king, even a symbolic death would mean a dissolution of the power structure with which he identifies himself. So he attempts to annihilate the prophecy of the 13th Wise Woman by wiping out all the spinsters in his kingdom for they are messengers of death. The story tells us that the king resorts to this scheme to protect his child, which is every responsible parent's primary concern, but can we help suspecting that on some level his actions are driven by patriarchy's deep-seated fear of feminine nature with its inherent mortality and revolutionary force?

Thorn-Rose's prolonged sleep is a gestation period which allows the menarcheal girl to flower, unperturbed by ceaseless intrusions from the rapacious masculine that covets and exploits the treasures of feminine nature. With anticipation, we await her awakening to new times where androgynous Love reigns supreme.

The Prince as Incarnation of a New Masculine Principle

We cannot leave Thorn-Rose without mentioning the prince, for this is his initiation tale also. The old man incarnates the archetype of the *wise old man* who guides the prince on his spiritual path. He is the masculine counterpart of the spinster, who attends to Thorn-Rose's crossing over into adulthood in the tower. He kindles the curiosity of the young man who is seized by uncontrollable desire to *see* the beautiful princess—to behold her. The old man's dissuasion only intensifies the spirit of the courageous hero who is prepared to venture through the thornhedge in order to lay eyes on Thorn-Rose. The prince's intent towards Thorn-Rose has the feel of reverence rather than the will to victory that typifies the mythical hero's conquest of the maiden who dwells within the boundaries of her sacred sanctuary, as exemplified by Skírnir's aforementioned wooing of Gerd on behalf of the fertility god Freyr. The prince, who awakens Thorn-Rose, incarnates a new masculine principle that has evolved out of a long period of trial and error as manifested by the vain attempts of those who went before. Now the moment is ripe. The blossoming thornhedge opens up to him, and he is led toward the blissful and invigorating source of Love.

In the Icelandic version of the story, the prince is said to have "drunk his wedding to Thorn-Rose." This archaic expression has roots in a Celtic ritual in which a new king wed himself to the goddess of the land, Lady Sovereignty, by drinking from a cup offered him by a queen who was her representative. Thorn-Rose is thus an incarnation of the goddess from whom the prince accepts his rulership as a new king who brings a new order to the collective.

It is said that when we follow our conviction wholeheartedly, life supports us. The prince is in the right place at the right time, and he dares follow his instinct without hesitation, even if his act seems a folly in the eyes of the world. Sometimes we find ourselves in such a situation and then it is futile to pause and debate with oneself—"should I or shouldn't I?"—for when we finally come to a conclusion, the magic moment has passed. It is, rather, a question of being attuned to one's instincts and daring to trust one's inner voice.

As children, we most likely saw the prince as a savior who released the helpless girl from an evil spell. We understood the story literally, and thus it affirmed the familiar myth about the weak and the strong sex. We are products of a civilization in which the goal has been to lord over nature and its rhythms and subject it to the interests of the ruling powers. This is why women have been steered from their creative power source while their role as wives and mothers has been exalted. The stories of the Valkyrie Brynhild and that of the giant maiden Gerd, which loom in the background of this tale, illustrate patriarchy's unyielding effort to subjugate the strong, independent female.

As children we may have commiserated with the 13th Wise Woman for having been left out. To be excluded is a chilling experience that some of us may have known. We feel unloved and inadequate. Thorn-Rose was her opposite. She was kind and everybody's favorite. She was perfection incarnate. She was who we would have wanted to be. We bought into the spell of the tale. We thought we were immortal and abhorred the curse of the 13th Wise Woman. We knew nothing about menstruation even though once a month our mothers bled under our noses. The "mortal wound" inside us had been a secret carefully hidden away. How were we to know that the child in us had to die to give way to the sexually ripe adult ushered in by menstruation? This is the Thorn-Rose whom the prince sees in full glory. In the incubation time allotted by the 12th Wise Woman the menarcheal girl is given time to mature. She is no longer the daughter of a father who controls her. She is a descendant of Lady Sovereignty, who in conjunction with her lover inaugurates a new era.

But what does it say that the hedge closed behind the prince again? Does it mean that what we witness is an inner marriage? That inner harmony is the cornerstone of a happy life? As Thorn-Rose is a collective tale of enduring popularity, one would guess that it contains a solution to a universal problem.

The Fairy Tale as a Dream

If we approach the tale as a dream, we might say that the personages it puts on stage embody rivaling powers in the dreamer's psyche. On the one hand is the cultural indoctrination imparted by parents and education, but on the other hand are the unconscious powers that call for a change because the present state of affairs has become petrified and blocks the creative evolution of the dreamer. Thorn-Rose and the prince would then be symbolic presentations of the opposite energies that animate every person, male or female. On the one hand, is the introvert and receptive stance incarnated by Thorn-Rose, but on the other hand is the aggressive and outgoing attitude personified by the prince. In fact, we get a glimpse of the latter in the girl child when she approaches the spinster and without further ado grasps the spindle from her hands. The fact that her finger then bleeds suggests that menstruation is seen as having a phallic, aggressive, connotation. This is again mirrored in the intrusion of the 13th Wise Woman.

What the story intimates is that the child is whole in herself, but with the onset of menstruation, the aggressive part becomes "the other" who needs to be "tamed" in interaction with the conscious personality. What is called for is a balanced rhythm between those opposite tendencies. We must not forget ourselves in the world of dreams nor should we take control of our nature with mindless cruelty. It is the prince's reverent attitude toward the feminine that earns him the healing love of his "other." This is a repeated lesson brought to us by fairy tales and folk tales. Whether nature works with or against us, depends on our intent and attitude toward it.

Red Rose

The red rose is a symbol of the love that endows our earthly lives with a poetic dimension. It is a symbol of the passions that drive us along the path toward spiritual growth, as exemplified by Freyja who cried tears of red-gold while seeking her departed husband *Od* ("poem, poetry"). The thorns are unavoidable companions on this journey. By opening our hearts to love and by following our hearts in search of spiritual truth rather than submitting blindly to creed, we risk being hurt. In our tale the thorn-rose is a symbol for the bleeding vulva. In Christian symbolism, the red rose stood for the blood shed by Jesus on the cross.[28] Jesus was a revolutionary who departed from the ruling principle of his day. His path to spiritual rebirth was marked by a crown of thorns and a bleeding wound, a symbolic vulva through which the church, his bride, was born. As in the menstruating female, we see the androgyny of the rose revealed in the male Christ. The thread that runs consistently

---

28   Biederman, p. 289.

between them unveils the spiritual dimension of menstruation. It is the *prima materia*, the "raw matter," which the conscious woman can transform into spiritual gold in attunement with her nature.

4
The "Hidden Woman" in Hafnanúpur

from Icelandic Folk and Fairy Tales, III

collected by Jón Árnason

The farm *Hafnir* was a fishing station in earlier times and is located in the northern part of Iceland, more precisely on the northernmost tip of the *Skagi*-peninsula. *Hafnir* is a plural word that means "ports". The peak Hafna*núpur* and the river Hafna*á* derive their names from this location.

In the early 18th century, a farmer by the name of Sigurd lived at Hafnir on Skagi. He had a wife by the name of Thurídur. They had four children. Their sons were named Bjarni, Jón, and Óttar; and their daughter Thorunn. The brothers were all of a boisterous temper and had a somewhat heathen streak. Their sister was very pretty, courteous, and skillfull. She was gentle and kind so that everybody loved her dearly, and she was considered to possess, in every respect, the qualities of an ideal wife.

One autumn, so it is said, she was looking for her father's lambs. She did not find the lambs, and when night had fallen and darkness set in she decided to turn back home. She walked along Hafnanúpur, on the eastern side. Looking at a belt of crags in the peak, she sees[1] an open door in the rock. Light burns on a lamp by a bed in this abode, and a handsome woman, clad in blue, sits on a chair near the light. She was doing needlework and looked out to Thorunn with a friendly mien, but the maiden was overcome with fear and took to her feet as fast as she could. Nonetheless she looked back. Then she felt that the woman sent her a wrathful glance and at that the door closed. Now Thorunn got lost and did not make it home that evening. The next day she was searched for but was not found. On the third day, she was at last found by a river called Hafnaá. There she lay asleep or in some sort of a trance. She was then transported home, but when she awoke she was half-deranged and her face distorted. She never became the same as before, neither as regarded her looks nor temperament.[2]

---

1   At this point in the tale there is a change to the present tense as if the storyteller endeavors to bring the experience of the wonder up close, to enter the tale and bring it to life. This is a common feature in Jón Árnason's collection as the tales have been written down verbatim from the oral sources.

2   The event related here is said to be true.

INTERPRETATION

The Hidden Dimension

"The 'Hidden Woman' in Hafnanúpur" is a folk tale, and as is stated in a footnote, the event it describes is said to be true. There is no visible blood in this tale, so why is it included in a collection that focuses on menstrual symbolism? In the introduction to my interpretation of "Thorn-Rose," I reflected on the secrecy that has surrounded menstruation and how that secrecy inevitably carried over into the tales. Today the taboo may seem to have been lifted, but do we stop to think about the meaning of menstruation and why, like Eve's unclean children, it has been so thoroughly hidden in our culture? Does the "hidden woman" hold a key to these questions? Who is she? What is her secret?

In "Genesis of 'Hidden People'" the spirits hidden in nature are in fact traced to Eve's unclean children:

> *God almighty once came to Adam and Eve. They received him with hospitality and showed him every nook and cranny of their house. They also showed him their children and he found them promising. He asked Eve if she did not have more children than those whom she had shown to him. She said no. But the truth was that Eve had not finished bathing some of the children and was ashamed to let god see them so she hid them away. God knew this and says [sic]: "What is intended to be hidden from me shall also be hidden from men." These children now became invisible to men and lived in mounds and hills, knolls and stones. This is the origin of elves but men are descended from the children whom Eve showed to god. Humans can never see elves unless they want to be seen for they can see men and make men see them.[3]*

---

3   Árnason, I, p. 7.

Not surprisingly, Eve is responsible for having peopled nature with unclean spirits. She tries to hide her shame from god and resorts to lying when confronted by his all-knowingness. I cannot resist speculating whether the god in this tale is a spokesman for the males who were excluded from the women's bower way back when!

It seems to me that what we can infer from "The 'Hidden Woman' in Hafnanúpur" is that it is up to us to redeem Eve's unclean descendants or that which we find shameful in ourselves. I imagine that if they want to be seen, they desire to be integrated into our consciousness to fill in the gaps in the unfinished picture we humans have created of the world.

Archetypes and the Collective Unconscious

In the last chapter, I explored Sibylle Birkhäuser-Oeri's suggestion that images and motifs in fairy tales conceal a meaning not immediately obvious. The search for that meaning is an archeological expedition through ancestral tales that point the way to the primitive part of us, which Birkhäuser-Oeri defines as a source of vitality and creativity. Susan Kim touches on the concealment in fairy tales of tabooed issues like menarche, menstruation, and a girl's transition into sexual adulthood. Referring to Bruno Bettelheim's view of fairy tales as a tool for teaching kids how to deal with issues like these, she says: "This does not mean it's overt; trust me, you'll be searching the Brothers Grimm until hell freezes over if you're looking for specific references to the endometrium, follicle-stimulating hormones, or Fallopian tubes."[4] So, like the "hidden woman" in the mountain peak, Thorunn's initiation into womanhood is in my view hidden in the images and motif of this tale.

---

4   Obtained 1/16/2015 on http://www.huffingtonpost.com/susan-kim/fairy-tales-child-develop_b_397620.html

Carl Jung discovered in the dreams of his patients motifs and symbols that had parallels in religions, myths, and tales of ancient and distant cultures, of which these dreamers could not possibly have had any knowledge. This discovery led to his theory of the archetypes and the collective unconscious, according to which we humans share certain fundamental patterns of instinctive behavior. At one point, Jung defined *archetype* as "an inherited tendency of the human mind to form representations of mythological motifs."[5] While those representations retain a basic pattern, they can vary a great deal as they take their guise and coloring from the individual consciousness in which they appear. The spinster in the tower whom Thorn-Rose addresses fearlessly as "mother" and the woman in the peak from whom Thorunn flees in terror are cases in point. Rising out of humanity's common ground, the collective unconscious, the archetypes connect us to the psychic life of our ancestors as far back as the earliest beginnings. In that sense, they can be said to function like a grounding mechanism in the vicissitudes of our human life. If we are estranged from our roots, we cannot flower. Such was the fate of the protagonist of our tale. To understand her reaction and tragic experience, we need to take her cultural background into consideration. But first let us look briefly at the etiology of folk tales and other archetypal stories.

Folk Tale versus Fairy Tale

In the last chapter, I referred to Marie-Louise von Franz's theory that archetypal stories originate most frequently "through individual experience of an invasion by some unconscious content, either in a dream or in a waking hallucination."[6] As is exemplified by our folk tale, an invasion of this sort is a numinous and unsettling experience.

---

5   http://aras.org/

6   1996, p. 24.

A supernatural event would have aroused curiosity and been spread by word of mouth and as the story circulated, it became amplified by other folkloric material that fit its context. Von Franz likens this development to that of rumors. "The 'Hidden Woman' in Hafnanúpur" accords well with her description. The tale is said to be grounded in an individual experience but has seemingly been amplified by formulas and mythological motifs, maybe in an attempt to explain the incomprehensible change in the young woman's character.

The folk tale differs from the fairy tale in that it revolves around a personal experience in a defined place and time. In the fairy tale, the hero is stereotyped, either black or white, while in the folk tale the protagonist is very human, and her experience of the uncanny is saturated with feeling. We see this difference in Thorn-Rose and Thorunn, both of whom I consider to be informed by the archetype of a girl's initiation into womanhood.

In order to understand Thorunn's mindset, we need to look at the cultural situation at the time of her dismal experience. In the *History of Icelandic Literature*, the 18th century is described thus: "The emphasis in religious books and sermons was on god's ire. According to those, nature was poisonous and filled with temptations, repulsive and dangerous, prey to satan and his devils."[7] The previous century had been marked by burnings of sorcerers at the stake. The writings of the Reverend Páll Björnsson (1621-1706), who was in the forefront of carrying out those punishments, are descriptive of the collective and pervasive fear of the devil who "churns up the lust of our corrupt nature so that, asleep or awake, we might drown in the dirt of our flesh."[8] With this historical stage in mind, we can imagine the terror of a young girl who found herself in the dark, literally and metaphorically, as she came face to face with her feminine nature.

---

7   Sæmundsson, p. 26.

8   P. 81.

Symbolism of the Lamb

The tale takes us right into the traditional patriarchal society of its time ("In the early 18th century a farmer by the name of Sigurd lived...") holding aloft the ideal of the charitable and loving maiden, while at the same time, being threatened by feminine nature. Thorunn's formulaic character description is almost identical with that of Thorn-Rose's. Before she met the "hidden woman" she was an exemplary girl, brought up to become a competent and compliant wife.

Thorunn is searching for her father's lambs the evening of the apparition. She does not find the lambs, gets lost herself, is searched for but is not really found again for she is no longer who she was. There is an underlying parallel between Thorunn and the lambs. The lamb is a virginal image. White, young, and graceful, it is a symbol of innocence and purity. In the Christian context, the lamb is a symbol for Christ. In early Christian iconography, the lamb took the place of the body of Christ on the cross, the innocent sacrificed for our sins. Sometimes it appears "stretched on the ground, with blood flowing."[9] In the shadow of this image, Thorunn, an innocent maiden who has become victim of feminine nature, lies in a coma by a *river* that bears the name of the "hidden woman's" peak. To the poets of old, for whom the earth was a living being, a river was the "blood of the earth." This poetic paraphrase may be our key to the menstrual theme hidden in this tale.

Ymir's Blood

According to Norse mythology, the sea and the lakes were made from the blood of the primordial frost-giant, Ymir, from whose dismembered body Odin and his two brothers created their

---

9   Charbonneau-Lassay, p. 74.

world. The sacrifice, on which Odin's reign was built, bears a close resemblance to the natural process of menstruation in which the potential embryo of a new life dissolves and flows out of the female body in a stream of blood:

> *In primitive view the embryo of a new life is "built up" from the blood, which ceases to flow during pregnancy (Neumann: 1991, 31). By the same token, menstruation spells death and dissolution of structure. It thus becomes the germinating soil of a new cycle of possibilities. It carries an evolutionary force which mythology gives us reason to believe thrust humanity out of a state of unconsciousness.*[10]

The male gods seemingly appropriated the natural process inherent in the female body, turning it into an act of volition. Thereby, a previous worldview founded on the female experience became overridden by that of the hero, whose objective was to conquer and submit nature to his interests. As storytelling was a traditional diversion in every farmhouse while people occupied themselves with handwork such as spinning, weaving, or woodcarving, we can take it for granted that Thorunn had been fed on stories of progressive heroes battling perilous nature where the end justified the means. Her very name is testimony to this heritage. In baptism she was consecrated to Thor, a god who was a sworn enemy of giantesses—and giantesses, we know, had their abodes in mountain caves. You will remember his bragging quoted in Chapter I: "I went east / and I battered giants / evil brides, / who went to the rock."[11] I rather suspect that the Thor we have come to know from mythology would have been no friend of the blue-clad woman in the rock. Further reflecting her culture's deeply rooted veneration of the heroic, her mother's name Thurídur means "she who is loved by Thor" and her father was named after "the greatest hero of all times," Sigurd "the dragon-slayer."

---

10   From my text on "Menstruation" in *The Book of Symbols: Reflections on Archetypal Images*, pp. 402-403.

11   *Hárbarðsljóð* ("Lay of Harbard"), st. 23.

If we accept Jung's definition that the archetype links us to the earliest beginnings of our ancestors' psychic life, we can assume that female initiation connects back to the first bleeding, when woman awakened to her intimate and rhythmic relationship with the moon. This psychic experience is, in my belief, the basis of the myth about Freyja's acquisition of Brísingamen which I suggested was a symbol inspired by the eclipse of the sun, when the heavenly bodies of the sun and the moon unite in intercourse and the solar prominences whirl around the black disk of the moon like a flaming necklace (see Pages 3 & 25). In Freyja's descent into the stone, this heavenly union was brought down to earth as she retraced humanity's steps back to the cave and surrendered herself to the four dwarfs in exchange for the treasure.

As Thorunn *happens* to see into the rock where the blue-clad woman is doing needlework, so the stone in which the dwarfs were forging the gold necklace *happened* to be open when Freyja came by and was immediately attracted to the piece. Freyja's foreknowledge— her gift as a *völva* who was able to see the connection between the past and the future—is evident in this description. She instinctively knew that her initiation into the mystery of the blood would lead her to spiritual wholeness and she dared trust her instinct. Thorunn, on the other hand, is of two minds. Her immediate impression of the blue-clad woman is a favorable one, but then fear takes hold of her and she runs away from her destiny. The tale intimates that her misfortune is brought about by her looking back. This is when she meets the wrathful eye of the "hidden woman" and loses her directions. But no more than her father's precautions could protect Thorn-Rose from the prick of the spindle, could Thorunn have escaped the symbolic sting of the "hidden woman's" needle.

In *Völuspá* ("Prophecy of the Seeress"), the *völva* recites a long list of dwarf names, beginning with *Nýi* and *Niði*, which refer to the crescent moon in the first and the last quarter respectively, followed by *Nordri* and *Sudri*, *Austri* and *Vestri*, names which correspond to the four cardinal directions. The four dwarfs with whom Freyja had intimate relations suggest wholeness as reflected in the completed circle of the moon. This circle motif is played upon by the double-entendre of the word *men* which refers both to the "moon" and the "necklace." In the tale it is emphasized that, when she came to the stone, the dwarfs were in the process of forging the necklace and that, in fact, it was about to be finished. This suggests that Freyja goes underground in the last and the dark phase of the moon that is framed by the crescents. On the one hand is the sickle moon as harbinger of death, on the other, the new crescent as a symbol of rebirth. In between is found the dark mystery, which would have referred to the cold world of dark Nifl in the North. In Iceland, when we want to send someone to hell, we yell at them "go North and under!" By putting the dwarf associated with the North first, the *völva* seems to emphasize its importance as the place of beginnings and endings in everlasting cyclicity.

Going back to the source, means going back to the quickening of Ymir which, according to myth, took place in the perfectly still Gap of Ginnungar (Ice. Ginnungagap) and was caused by a drip engendered by the meeting of rime blasting from the cold and dark world of Nifl in the North and a hot breeze blowing from the fiery world of Múspell in the South. As in the solar eclipse, we have the merging of opposites brought about by Spirit in the guise of frosty gusts on the one hand and a hot breeze on the other. *Ginnungar* means "fools." This suggests that the Gap of Ginnungar betokens a state of being that holds an attraction.

In *Völuspá*, the *völva* describes Ymir's dwelling before the beginning (in my literal translation): "There was no sea nor cool waves, no earth nor a heaven, there was the gap of Ginnungar but grass nowhere."[12] Out of this nothingness, the world unfolds

---

12 St. 3.

in cocreation with human consciousness. This is the birthplace of feeling, of any new idea. But why would those who feel attracted to this place beyond differention have been called *ginnungar*?

Coming from the mouth of a *völva* who was a familiar in this timeless zone, which she needed to access in order to fulfill her function, I feel tempted to read into this attribution the positive meaning of The Fool as an archetype, that is, someone who journeys with an open mind, without prejudgments, into an alien world to obtain the magical means which will heal her or his community (see image).

From another point of view, the name Gap of Ginnungar was most likely intended as a deterrent against letting oneself be lured. As opposed to fairy tales, which are a spontaneous product of the unconscious, a myth is condoned by the establishment and intended to educate. This would most likely have been the understanding Thorunn had in her blood. I can imagine what must have flashed through her mind when she encountered the "hidden woman": *Don't let yourself be fooled by appearances! She may seem to be friendly, but in reality it is the devil out to get you!* I strongly suspect that the gold necklace that exerted an attraction on Freyja and earned her the reputation of a whore was considered to be such a lure. In fact, I would not be surprised if her acquisition of the treasure inspired this dubious naming to deter women from following in her footsteps. But stealing it from her by tricks and deceit was a sign of man's cleverness in his commerce with feminine nature.

Going into rocks suggests primal engagement with matter and the body. The gold necklace points to the value of the blood as the *prima materia*,[13] the first material in which was embedded the promise of the gold as an indestructible metal and symbol of the highest spiritual

---

13   Robert Place defines the *Materia Prima* (first material) thus: "the single, invisible, indestructible substance, from which all things derive and to which all things return" (55).

THE FOOL

attainment. I refer again to Philalethes, who claimed that alchemists were in possession of a know-how for "extracting the Royal Diadem from the menstrual blood of a whore" (see Page 7). This gives us a clue as to why Freyja's Brísingamen was of such importance to Odin and why he felt that he needed to take control of the energy inherent in the precious substance. The Royal Diadem to which the alchemists aspired one suspects would refer to the crown of Christ as King who unifies the masculine and the feminine in himself. This might explain the thread that one detects between the menstruating female and the redeemer whose blood was shed on the cross for our sins. The underlying parallel between Thorunn and the lamb as a sacrificial victim seems to hint at this connection.

As the end result is embedded in the *prima materia*, so the body is simultaneously a cave and a heavenly mansion. Our ancestors lived in a unified world, and it seems that the purpose of our journey is to consciously reclaim and integrate our original wholeness. *Ymir* means "twin." It is a masculine name but reflects the primordial being's androgynous nature. Ymir is the Sun and the Moon, the conscious and the unconscious in a dissolving embrace. In him the opposites unite, the quick and active principle of fire and the slow and passive principle of matter (ice), often labeled respectively as the masculine and the feminine. The verb *ymja* which refers to "sound" and is often used in connection with water, such as the deep sound of the ocean or the rumbling of a waterfall, has been associated with *Ymir* and endows the monumental awakening with a musical connotation.

I understand the awakening of Ymir as a metaphor for the sparking of divine Love in the human heart; the meeting of opposites in the middle of the unfathomable abyss of human potential as desire awakens the mind and launches evolution. What was frozen and immobile is awakened by the Spirit of Love. This is when the greening begins. We saw this in Thorn-Rose's awakening. And we emphasized that to merit its name, Love is necessarily all-inclusive and the opposite of self-interest.

In her search of her wild-spirit husband Od, I picture Freyja as the archetypal Fool, open to the experiences that come her way as she plunges into the Gap of Ginnungar, trusting that the ground will rise to meet her feet at every step:[14]

> *Od went far away, but Freyja stays behind and cries, but her tear is red-gold. Freyja has many names, but this is because she assumed various names when she journeyed amongst foreign peoples in search of Od.*[15]

One scholar remarks that "in this passage Snorri does not explain how Freyja both remains at home and wanders in search of Od."[16] I suggest that Freyja's journeys took place during seclusion in her firmly locked bower at the end of which she bore her insights out into the world! Driven by love of the Other, Freyja is every woman's guiding star in her quest for wholeness.

Menstruation and the Mead of Poetry

In Snorri's *Edda* we find this disavowal of Ymir put into Odin's mouth: "By no means do we acknowledge him as God. He was evil and all his descendants, we call them frost-giants. And it is said that when he slept he got blood."[17] We have seen that sleep is frequently associated with menstruation, which brings the body into focus and tends toward union of mind and matter. When Thorn-Rose has pricked her finger, she falls immediately asleep and Thorunn, after her encounter with the "hidden woman," was found asleep or in some sort of trance by the river. In a hero's tale, on the other hand, sleep equals unconsciousness and is the opposite of discrimination

---

14   "Wherever he [The Fool] goes, the ground rises to meet his feet" (Amberstone, Lesson 1).

15   Snorri Sturluson. "Gylfaginning", ch. 35.

16   MacCulloch, p. 125.

17   "Gylfaginning," ch. 5.

and action. These opposite tendencies would inevitably have caused a conflict in the ancestral androgynous Ymir. What is called for is balance. But somewhere along the evolutionary road humanity lost sight of the golden medium. The heroic spirit, associated with the masculine, has been exalted to the skies in our Western culture while feminine nature, revered by our distant ancestors, has been dethroned, and to an extent driven underground and demonized. "The 'Hidden Woman' in Hafnanúpur" is testimony to this development and its dire consequences for women and the human condition in general. When twelve pastors' wives in "The Witch's Ride" (Chapter 6) offer their menstrual blood to Satan in return for magical wisdom, we suspect an underlying connection between the lord of darkness and the ancient frost-giant, deprecated by Odin in the above quote.

Snorri is being sarcastic when he attributes the above disavowal to Odin for in reality he is alluding to Odin's theft of the mead of poetry which elevated him to the status of a solar-hero and All-Father. By his deed, Odin usurped the place of his parent, "the old giant." There exist two versions of the myth about the theft of the precious mead: one attributed to Odin himself in *Hávamál* ("Sayings of the High One") and a prose version in Snorri's *Edda*. According to the latter, Odin gulped down the entire supply of the mead and ferried it in the shape of an eagle to Asgard, the celestial abode of the gods. In the poem, it seems like he got away with the vessel itself. The eclipse of the sun, which I believe inspired the idea of Freyja's Brísingamen as a symbol for the "red-gold" lacing the neck of the womb, has also been described as a chalice: "At the solar eclipse... the shadow of the moon on the sun can make [...] a bright grail containing a dark drink."[18] It would seem that Brísingamen and the elixir coveted by Odin are of the same substance and a metaphor for the unified opposites of spirit and matter in a place beyond time.

---

18   Shuttle and Redgrove, p. 190.

The mead of poetry was kept in Hnitbjörg under the guardianship of Gunnlöd, a giant maiden and daughter of Suttungr to whom Odin refers as "the old giant" in the poem. The name *Hnitbjörg* evokes a secret mountain dwelling which opens and closes automatically and contains a treasure of some sort. We have already seen this magic at work in the tale about Freyja and the dwarfs and in Thorunn's vision of the blue-clad woman in the mountain peak. Unlike them, Odin was not being invited. According to Snorri's version, he tricked his way into the rocky abode in the shape of a snake. Snorri provides us with food for exploring the kinship between the snake and the dwarfs. The latter, he says, were the first sparks of life in the earth and underground. They quickened in the flesh of Ymir as worms but through the agency of the gods became carriers of mnemonic wisdom and took on the shape of men, yet they live in the earth and stones.[19] What we see is an evolution of primary instinct toward humanization which opened the door to interaction between body and mind. Louis Charbonneau-Lassay describes how the ancient world "saw in the snake, born of the Earth-Mother from whom it comes forth renewed each springtime, the image of life. Coming from the earth, the snake was considered the knower of all its secrets, and this is why the oldest legends made it, like the dragon, the guardian of all sorts of hidden riches: the treasures of metals, of medical cures, and of magic."[20] Dwarfs, too, were guardians at the threshold between worlds. We saw this in Freyja's descent and the price the dwarfs exacted from her for the necklace which gave her access to the source of divine wisdom. They were metal workers and forgers of magical tools and weapons and carriers of unlimited wisdom to boot, as is exemplified by *Alvís*, the "omniscient" dwarf who burst into the halls of Thor and claimed the god's daughter as his bride (see Page 27 ff).

---

19   "Gylfaginning," ch. 14.

20   P. 155.

As Ymir came about through the merging of fire and ice, so the cold-blooded serpent unifies in itself the opposites of spirit and matter: "A serpent flows like water and so is watery, but its tongue continually flashes fire."[21] This would have been seen as a transforming cohabitation made visible in the snake's rejuvenating itself in shedding its old skin, a trait it shares with the womb that sheds its lining in menstruation as does the moon shed its old self during its dark phase and is ever reborn. Judith Grahn points out that "Western minds have been taught to see the snake as penile" although when swallowing food it looks more like a vagina.[22] By the same token dwarfs are presented exclusively as male in Norse mythology. Thus they do not reproduce nor does the womb conceive during menstruation. However, the tale about Freyja's acquisition of Brísingamen indicates that the dwarfs inseminated her with the germ of spiritual wholeness as depicted in the gold necklace. It also implies that the period, when woman withdrew from her mundane duties, was considered an auspicious time for communion with Spirit. We remember that Freyja's encounter with the dwarfs followed on the heels of the description of her firmly locked bower into which no man was allowed without her consent. Hnitbjörg, that secret mountain dwelling that welcomes those who are in alliance with nature but does not invite those who are not, may be derived from the same motive.

Archeological findings do reveal an intimate relationship between the goddess and the snake. This intimacy is brought up close by Shuttle and Redgrove who refer to "reports that the Sibyls, just as they allowed temple snakes to lick into their ears to clear them for prophecy, allowed each snake their first seep of blood at the cervix," and they suggest that "this intimate and to us almost inconceivable event would have had a religious and probably shamanistic, that is,

---

21 Campbell, p. 47.

22 P. 58.

a creative purpose."[23] In *Hávamál* ("Sayings of the High One"), Odin relates that Gunnlöd, sitting on a golden chair,[24] gave him a sip of the precious mead. The parallels between the Norse myth where Odin assumes the shape of a snake to get to the mead and the above description of the Greek oracle would seem to suggest that Gunnlöd was a priestess and an instrument of the divinity. Odin's theft of the mead of poetry may thus be another version of Apollo's takeover of the oracle at Delphi which had previously been dedicated to Gaia, the earth goddess. The fact that the sibyls could be consulted only on one day of the month, may indicate, as Shuttle and Redgrove suggest, that their prophesying was connected to their menses. In which case Odin would have been after Gunnlöd's menstrual blood, as in fact seems to be confirmed by his declaration below.

Having insinuated himself into Gunnlöd's sanctuary under the pretense of an intimate, that is, a snake, Odin lay with her for three nights, and she allowed him one sip of the precious mead for each night. In the poem, Odin ruefully admits that he repaid Gunnlöd with ill for her "wholeheartedness." He acknowledges having betrayed Suttungr, Gunnlöd's father, by depriving him of his drink and caused Gunnlöd to cry. We are reminded of Freyja's tear of red-gold. When Odin has returned with his booty from this dangerous journey, during which he risked losing his head,

---

23   P.148.

24   *Priestess of Delphi* (1891) by John Collier shows the Pythia sitting on a high golden tripod draped in a cascading red shawl (http://en.wikipedia.org/wiki/Pythia). It was Svava Jakobsdottir, author of *Gunnlaðar saga* ("Saga of Gunnlöd"), who pointed out that it was Gunnlöd who sat on the golden chair, not Odin, as had been uncritically accepted before. From a grammatical point of view it is the more logical interpretation. With reference to Celtic tradition, where a king accepts his power from a goddess, Lady Sovereignty, or her representative who serves him a ritual cup of mead and has intercourse with him, Svava sees Gunnlöd as a representative of the goddess of the land from whom Odin accepted his power as king. Scholars have generally read the two texts together to fill in the gaps in one or the other and make the story fuller. Svava's interpretation is however confined to the poem. Menstrual power does not come into play in her interpretation. She however emphasizes that the drink in the Irish initiation ritual of the king is red, and is in fact identified with that color, and extremely potent to boot.

that is, his consciousness, he declares, in rather obscure language which nonetheless seems to conceal an important clue (in my literal translation): "A well bought color / I have well enjoyed / not much does the wise lack..."[25]. He does not specify which color he is referring to. The idea of his "buying a color" has had scholars perplexed to the extent that some believe the verse to be distorted beyond salvaging.[26] The Icelandic word for color is *litur* and coincidentally *Litur* is the name of a dwarf. The dwarfs, who according to Snorri quickened in the flesh of Ymir as snakes, we now know were intimately linked with the "red-gold" as forgers of Freyja's Brísingamen, and in particular Nordri who was associated with the cold North and the dark phase of the moon. It looks like on his regressive journey into the womb of the earth mother, Odin, a renowned shapeshifter, assumed the shape of the dwarf Litur, that first spark of life in the earth.

I venture that what Odin was after was "the menstrual blood of a whore" from which the alchemists endeavored to extract the Royal Diadem. In alchemy, the transforming solvent is referred to as *tincture*, i.e. color. And as the Philosophers' Stone itself, the panacea and ultimate goal of the Great Work, the tincture is red.[27] By taking control of this transforming power that belongs to woman, Odin endeavored to mold her to suit his ends. He stresses that he "bought" this color, this tincture, which endows him with wisdom. He thereby implies that Gunnlöd was a whore who let herself be bought. And this, in fact, became the fate of woman, to be a merchandise exchanged between father and husband whose property she became, body and

---

25   St. 107.

26   Svava Jakobsdottir believes that color (*litur*) is here a reference to the Irish ceremonial drink served the king to be. She says that its color is emphasized to the point that the drink is literally named after its color, *derg flaith*, which means "the red ale" (1988, p. 225). Gísli Sigurdsson (1998) believes that *litur* refers to Gunnlöd as in an earlier stanza (93) Odin talks about *colors that arouse lust*. Such colors Gísli interprets as physical appearance. He compares the wording of the verse to the expression to "buy a wife" as some have seen the poem as an independent version of the story and interpret Odin's visit into the *halls of Suttungr* as a wooing journey.

27   Edinger, p. 72.

soul. Her sovereignty was quenched. This was the trend, which, unfortunately, we see still at work in the world. Thorunn, our tale stresses, was considered in every respect to possess the qualities of an ideal wife. Those were the high prospects her culture held up to her. Descriptions like this one suggest that to be marriageable was propagandized as a desirable quality that saved a girl from the pitiful lot of spinsterhood.

Odin's theft of the mead of poetry would have been the moment in time when Od, the husband Freyja searched for in pain and sorrow, disappeared from the stage and the female was cast in the role of a muse rather than that of a creator in her own right. The fact that the names Odin (Óðinn) and Od (Óðr) are synonymous suggest that Odin usurped the latter's role.

Suttungr, the old giant's name, may be related to Jutish *sutte* = "to come rushing" or Swedish *sutta* = "to soil, wet" and *sotta* = "splashing through water."[28] Do these meanings evoke the North Wind's frosty gusts stirring up instincts and emotions that have been buried in the unconscious? Such an experience can indeed feel like a chilling blow to the conscience. We might prefer not to deal with it and ban it from our consciousness. It is not for nothing that menstruation has been referred to as "The Moment of Truth."[29] It is also of interest in the context of our subject that the poets of old equated the "word or voice" of giants with gold.[30] They thus acknowledged that this was where their inspiration came from. Giants tend to be presented as simpletons because theirs is the voice of nature. Unlike the civilized man, they do not know how to lie. In the "Prophecy of the Seeress," the *völva* is

---

28   Magnússon, p. 990.

29   Annette Høst, who is a shaman, suggests that we call "PMS, the pre-menstrual syndrome, the horrible monster... The Moment of Truth!" She urges women to "listen to it, co-operate, and make creative use of it." And she emphasizes that "even though its language can be harsh sometimes, you can trust that it speaks to us from a deep, honest place" (http://www.shamanism. dk/blessedbymoon.htm).

30   "Skáldskaparmál" in Snorris Sturluson's *Edda*, ch. 46.

the bearer of bad news as she reveals to Odin that his reign, founded on betrayal, will collapse. At the end of the poem she announces that she will go under, as if she foresees that her truth speaking voice will be silenced. And so it was. And the lying continues.

A younger version of the name Suttungr is *Suptungur,* which is related to *súpa* = "sip."[31] The name of the vessel containing the mead was *Óðrerir* = "he who stirs up poetry." One cannot help but notice that the androgynous phenomena, Ymir and the vessel, which one would think refers primarily to the womb, are given masculine names. In like manner Suttungr is said to be Gunnlöd's father. This is testimony to the appropriation by the male of the spiritual fountain with which woman is graced through her biological make-up. The mother, the feminine part of the primal godhead, had receded into the shadows. She became a "hidden woman." This is reflected in the genealogy of the twins Freyja and Freyr, who are said to be the children of the fertility god Njord but a mother is nowhere mentioned.

Odin's acclaimed deed parallels Freyja's vilified adventure with the dwarfs in the stone that graced her with precious Brísingamen. Both events are descriptive of a dramatic shift in the history of human consciousness, but while Freyja's initiation was characterized by surrender to nature, Odin's initiation was marked by deceit and exploitation that left the fooled giant maiden crying behind. It was an act that was to have serious consequences for women. At this juncture, enmity replaced woman's harmonious relationship with her womb. Bölverkur, the name which Odin assumed on this heroic mission, is reflective of the adversity henceforth inflicted on woman by menstruation. *Bölverkur* is a composite word, the first part of which means "misfortune, cross (to bear)," and the latter "pain." Considering that it is the name of Odin as an agent in this drama, it also applies to his deed that brought woman's suffering about.

---

31   Magnússon, p. 990.

It is worth noticing that Bölverkur was a name Odin assumed himself. This goes hand in hand with the careful planning of his premeditated act as described by Snorri. In that his theft of the mead differed from Freyja's acquisition of Brísingamen which was revealed to her when she came to the stone, as does the "hidden woman" reveal herself to Thorunn. In those examples, the unconscious makes the first move and seeks to become an integrated part of consciousness. While Freyja surrenders herself to nature, Odin's act goes against nature and indicates that suffering is not a natural partner of menstruation. Menstruation happens to woman; will does not come into play. And so does the inspiration for a poem, an invention or a work of art. It seems that the menstrual moment was experienced as an auspicious time for receptivity of divine intervention into human affairs.

In her *Interior Castle* Teresa of Ávila (1515-1582) describes the "Spiritual Marriage" as a "secret union [that] takes place in the deepest centre of the soul, which must be where God Himself dwells."[32] We cannot go deeper than the place of origin, the cave. The exquisite sculpture *The Ecstasy of Saint Teresa* by Gian Lorenzo Bernini was inspired by Teresa's description of a visionary experience in which an angel, "not tall, but short" stood by her side with in his hand "a long golden spear, and at the point of the iron there seemed to be a little fire. This I thought that he thrust several times into my heart, and that it penetrated to my entrails." It was an experience, albeit painful, that left her "all on fire with a wondrous love for God."[33] As befits the subject, Bernini has fashioned the angel in the likeness of Eros, the god of love.

Do we detect a shadow of the serpent flashing its fiery tongue behind the image of the golden spear with fire at its point? Keeping

---

32   P. 215.

33   Moon, p. 219.

in mind Snorri's description of an evolutionary link between worms and dwarfs, maybe Teresa's vision of the angel whose face "shone as though he were one of the highest of the angels, who seemed to be all of fire" points to a kindred evolution of the primal image as a transforming agent, reflecting the stance and stage of development of the conscious personality. Saint Teresa was a mystic whose creative power found an influential outlet within her religious order and in the church, and she wrote numerous books that continue to speak to the reader of today. It may be of interest in the context of our subject that in the mundane sense Teresa was a *spinster* while in the religious sense she was the bride of Christ, a Bridegroom with whom she had a profound relationship.

Interestingly, Odin's attribute was a spear called *Gungnir* ("he who trembles or swings") with which he pierced himself, sacrificing himself to himself, when he hung fasting for nine nights in the world tree and obtained rune-wisdom. What was given naturally to Freyja, Odin had to quest for through pain and deprivation. This was both heroic and admirable, while *seiðr*, the ritual practiced by the *völva* to access the timeless zone of non-differentiation, became stigmatized as a *lower* type of magic and a shameful practice for men. Brísingamen and Gungnir would have been symbolic of the opposites inherent in the bisexual Ymir. Teresa emphasizes that God reveals Himself to the soul when He so pleases. The power is in God's hands. This would apply to the visions of Freyja and Thorunn but are we to understand Odin's sneaky act vis-à-vis Gunnlöd as a divine plan and a revelation? Was her pain of the same order as that of Teresa's? I find that hard to believe.

In a text dedicated to *The Ecstasy of Saint Teresa* it says that "the erotic nature of her mystical experience was initiatory and, as it were, impregnated her with her future career.'[34] Odin's deed robs

---

34   Ibid., p. 221.

Gunnlöd of her natural source of inspiration as he overtakes her mind. In *Hávamál* ("Sayings of the High One"), he describes how he extolled himself with great many words in the *halls of Suttungr*.[35] This attribution confirms that Hnitbjörg, the womb place in which Gunnlöd guarded the precious mead, was dedicated to the "old giant." What seems to be hinted at is that the giant maiden bought into Odin's convincing words much like Eve fell for the serpent's arguments in the Garden of Eden. Seated on her golden chair, she offered him a sip of the mead, but in his thirst for power he drank up. From now on, he was The All-Father who meted out the mead of poetry while Suttungr, who I believe referred to the spirit from the dark world of Nifl and the voice of Truth, became an enemy banned from the stage. And Odin did not give the mead to just anybody, he gave it to the *Æsir*, the gods of his pantheon, and to those men who knew how to compose poems.[36] The scarcity of the mention of female poets in our literary history makes one wonder whether there were any women among the lucky ones.[37]

Before Ymir's emergence, the Gap of Ginnungar was still "as if there was no breath of air."[38] It was as if creation held its breath and awaited in suspension for a numinous event to occur. Ymir was the response to that situation. We see this pattern repeated time and again in the history of mankind. Every new invention, every new theory seems to be born into such circumstances or else it would not capture attention and become integrated into the culture. Myth thus affirms *sub rosa* that the first bleeding and creation preceded the heroic act of Odin and his brothers who are held aloft

---

35   St. 104.

36   Snorri Sturluson. "Skáldskaparmál," ch. 6.

37   On March 26th 2014, the host of the literary program *Kiljan* took his viewers on a tour around Reykjavik to visit the statues that have been erected in the memory of Icelandic poets whom the establishment has recognized as worthy of such an honor. To emphasize the fact that there was not one woman amongst them, he faced his audience and asked: "Where are the women?"

38   Snorri Sturluson. "Gylfaginning," ch. 5.

as first creators. Somebody had to have been there to witness and channel the emergence of Ymir, whose primal status makes him the cornerstone of human culture. The brothers' dismemberment of Ymir signifies a dissolution of a pre-existing religious worldview. It symbolizes the solar hero's initial transgression on his bloody way to dominion over nature on all fronts. In an effort to subject woman to the solar hero, whose divine prototype was Odin All-Father, her spiritual relationship with her lunar nature was made ugly and fearful. But the archetype of female initiation takes us beyond that distortion and denigration. *Religion* means to "link back," from Lat. *religare*. Through religion we link back to our divine origin. But as is revealed in the tales that follow, the Church, as an official religious establishment, has been an impediment rather than a facilitator for women on their evolutionary road toward wholeness.

The "Hidden Woman"

Let us now turn to the "hidden woman." After all, the title of the tale implies that the story is essentially about her. When I first came across the myth about Odin's theft of the mead of poetry from Gunnlöd and saw that his exploit led to the paraphrasing of poetry as Odin's gain and *his* find, and *his* drink and *his* gift and the drink of the Æsir made available through *his* act, I was stunned. What about Gunnlöd, I asked myself. Where is she? What happened to her? I searched my books in vain. After this momentous event, Gunnlöd was dropped from myth. She had become a "hidden woman" nowhere to be found. I now wonder whether she has not returned to the stage of the human drama in this tale of female initiation.

The sacred mead was under Gunnlöd's guardianship in a cave, and the cave was a sacred place to the ancestors, symbolizing our origin and the womb of the earth-mother. The blue-clad woman in the rock seemingly personifies the archetype of the *spinster* whose unbroken thread leads back to the primal source.[39] She is the spiritual "grandmother"-figure of countless initiation tales who guides the young woman across the threshold into womanhood. At this moment the girl is in-between worlds as our tale demonstrates. Thorunn stands virtually on the threshold of a door leading into another dimension. She sees a light in the dark. She is being invited into the sacred place of female creativity, but she succumbs to fear and does not manage the transition. Some tribal societies will subject the initiate to a solitary quest for a dream or a vision that will point to her path in life. In those societies the community takes an active interest in the girl's experience and helps her channel it. But given the collective fear of a devil-possessed nature in Thorunn's culture, we can assume that she was caught without preparation and positive guideposts. She might have been familiar with the tale of Thorn-Rose, and certainly that of the Valkyrie Brynhild who was skilled with the needle, but the tragic fate of those heroines would have steered her from following in their footsteps.

By now we have become familiar with Freyja's bower and the widespread custom of menstrual seclusion. From the scant insights we get into the bower in the old sagas, we see women engaged in creative work, weaving, embroidery, song and poetry, and they would make themselves receptive to prophetic and healing dreams. The bed in the blue-clad woman's abode may suggest receptivity and repose from action.

---

39   In her foreword to *Women of the World: A Global Collection of Art*, a companion book to an exhibition featuring art by women from all over the world, Arlene Raven says of Mary Cassatt's painting *Lydia at a Tapestry Frame*: "The artist's sister stands as an example of her gender, class, and time. But Lydia at the spindle or stitching with a needle also holds an implicit symbolic meaning - woman as sacred female creativity, personified as the ancient Spinster" (p. 6).

Chaste Bride of Gods

Another mountain-dweller, all but *hidden* from view in the myths, is the goddess *Skadi* (a masculine noun meaning "damage"). The glimpses we get of her intimate a strong and independent female who knows what she wants. Skadi was a Valkyrie (see Chapter 3) and a daughter of a giant who was killed by the gods. Once married to the fertility god Njord, designated father and unique parent of Freyja and her twin brother Freyr, she split up with him and settled in the mountains where she runs on skis and hunts with bow and arrow. The very fact that Skadi is a masculine name for a female goddess hints at her androgynous nature, and its meaning, "damage," reveals that she had qualities that the patriarchy did not appreciate in a woman.

In the gods' punishment of Loki for bringing about the death of Baldr "the good," son of Odin, Skadi is identified with the venom-spewing snake while her counterpart, Loki's faithful and protective wife, Sigyn, is associated with the receptive bowl. When the gods had captured Loki, they bound him in a cave. Then Skadi took a serpent and fastened it up above him so that the venom dripped in his face but Sigyn stands by his side and holds a bowl under the dripping venom. When she goes to empty the bowl, Loki's seizures make the earth tremble. And there he will lie bound to the end of Odin's world.

The goddess' venomous aspect notwithstanding, etymology points to Lat. *scătĕre* "to gush forth" and *scătūrīgo* "a spring of bubbling water" as the source of Skadi's name. This would link back to the primal source, the coming into being of androgynous Ymir through the melting of ice by heat from sparking fire. And it brings to mind the river in our tale, which bears the name of the "hidden woman's" peak. In one Eddic poem Skadi is called "chaste bride of gods."[40] It is an attribute that may point to her status as a priestess.

---

40   *Grímnismál*, ("Lay of Grímnir"), st. 11.

The High Priestess on the Rider-Waite-Smith Tarot card (see image) is shown as a channel for the water of life streaming down from the moon with which she is crowned. Interestingly the image shows only three phases of the moon. The new moon, its dark phase, is hidden from view. I cannot help but wonder why. Would this go hand-in-hand with the "hidden woman's" exile from civilization? Is this exclusion analogous with Gunnlöd's and Skadi's disappearances from myth? She is seated on a stone cube between the pillars of darkness and light, of regressive and progressive energies. As the central pillar, it is she who weaves the opposites into a harmonious pattern. Her function as High Priestess is to ensure balance, to bar the human species from losing touch with its roots. Given the cultural situation in which Thorunn found herself, we can imagine that the blue clad woman in the cave appeared to her precisely for those reasons.

In her heart place the priestess has an even armed cross. This symbolizes cross roads, which is where a young girl being initiated into womanhood finds herself. At the center of the cross, where the horizontal line of time and the vertical line of timelessness intersect, the door that leads to the treasure opens up. What I see behind the priestess is a huge vase. Generally this is interpreted as a veil, but why, I ask myself, does it appear in the shape of a vase? I bet it is the vessel containing the precious mead that Gunnlöd guarded in the cave! The pattern on its outside reflects the fertilizing opposites it contains, pictured as womblike pomegranates and phallic palm trees, and those are arranged in the pattern of the Kabbalistic tree of life. In her lap, she holds, not an embroidery, but a closed scroll on which is written TORA. This is a reference to the Torah, the first five books of the Old Testament that open with the story of Eve's disobedience that caused man's fall from grace. It is a book that cannot be praised for celebrating woman's menstrual nature, which may explain why the black phase of the moon is not flaunted on this card. It is not altogether absent, though. Replacing it, I believe, is the priestess's raven black hair, symbolizing her occult powers.

THE HIGH PRIESTESS

Skadi's "spinsterhood" and lack of interest in physical relations with the opposite sex would have made her a bad example for young women on the threshold of womanhood. The word *spinster* as a denomination for an unmarried woman seems to still carry this stigma. Furthermore, Skadi's choice of residence on her father's domain in snow clad mountains and her skill with bow and arrow reflect spiritual aspirations and faithfulness to a religious worldview that antedates the heroic age when domestication of women became an important issue. Her hermitic inclinations and her love of the wild and unchartered was in direct opposition to this trend.

In the introduction to "Giants" in the collection of *Icelandic Folk and Fairy Tales*, it is stated that the denomination *giantess* and its various synonyms, shrew, hag, witch, and the like, are vilifications used about women who are in some way impetuous or unfeminine. This is the underside of the ideal maiden as prospective wife and mother that patriarchy has held up to women through the ages. Although women of today have become emancipated in myriad ways, Skadi is a shadow that we can still mine for gold.

The Cave Dweller's Dissolving Eye

The turning point in the tale occurs when Thorunn looks back. The woman's friendly look has turned hostile and Thorunn gets lost. In a progressive culture that aimed for immortality and the heavens, looking back would have implied regression to a more primitive state. The Bible holds aloft as a deterrent the story of Lot's wife who was turned to a pillar of salt for looking back to Sodom. Was it her looking back that caused Thorunn's fall from grace? Or was it caused by cultural indoctrination that blocked her from linking back to her roots at a crucial moment in her life? She is taken by surprise. There has been no guidance, apart from the church's denigration of nature intended to steer the flock toward salvation. Might not this very attempt have become Thorunn's doom? Jung has pointed out that the more severe the repression, the more archaic the unconscious content. We cannot go further back than the cave.

In Chapter 2, I mentioned Laurie Schapira's definition of the truth-seeing third eye as the "the dark vaginal eye of the goddess" and pondered whether Freyja's tear of red-gold might have been inspired by the red solar prominences whirling around the black lunar limb during an eclipse of the sun. There is a long tradition of associating the evil eye with menstruating women. When Pliny reports that if they happen to "go over a vessel of wine" it will sour, we suspect a veiled reference to the vaginal eye.[41] Freyja's tears celebrated as gold by the poets of old gave way to the fearful evil eye of giantesses who live in rocky mountains, exiled from civilization. Whoever meets the gaze of these powerful females either faints or drops dead. *Járngerd* ("she who is enclosed by an ironhedge") tops them all: "Any creature who comes before her eyes while she expires, will rot alive immediately."[42] A monster not easily done away with!

The Virgin and the Valkyrie

Our "hidden people" are generally dressed in blue and so is the Virgin Mary. When I was exploring this tale with a group of women, the blue-clad woman in the cave evoked Mary to some of them. It is true that Mary had gone underground in the religious life of the Icelandic people at this time. Annals relate that when Lutheranism replaced Catholicism in the mid-16th century, it was forbidden to believe in saints, whether it be Peter, Paul, Mary, or any other. Crosses and statues were destroyed, and burning a light in front of a saint was an act of violation. So at the time Thorunn had her encounter with the "hidden woman" seated by a light in a cave, the

---

41   Elder, p. 305.

42   Árnason, I, p. 241.

Mother had been exiled from the church and the flock was held in check by a retributive Father.

There is however an important difference between the blue-clad woman in the cave and the image we have of Mary, who is generally presented in the arts with her baby son in her lap. We do not see her engaged in creative work as is the "hidden woman."[43] As touched on above, there is a story that has been a living part of Icelandic culture through the ages and would certainly have been familiar to Thorunn, namely that of the Valkyrie Brynhild. Brynhild was engaged in needlework[44] when Sigurd "the dragon slayer" happened to see her

---

43   In the context of menstruation, the needle may be of significance. The needle stings, as did the spindle rod in Thorn-Rose, and so does a serpent's fang with which it paralyzes its victim. It is interesting to note that Loki's mother, Laufey, was also called *Nál*, meaning "needle." *Laufey* is a composite noun which means "leaf" and "island." Her double identity accords with the nature of her son who was both a *thurs* and a god. The fact that Loki was associated with his mother and called Laufeyjarson (son of Laufey) points to matriarchal roots.

44   Interpretations vary as to whether it was an embroidery or a weaving as the text is not clear about this: "She sat by a golden runner onto which she *read* my past and done deeds." When Brynhild finds out that she has been betrayed (see Page 54), she tears her runner apart in a fury. She brings about Sigurd's death and then kills herself in order to follow him to the beyond. What I find fascinating is how Bryndhild kills herself. She drives a sword "under her arm," i.e., into her side. And while she bleeds she offers gold to all who are present. Her wound would appear to be a prefiguration of the wound in the side dealt to Christ on the cross. Put into alchemical parlance, woman's blood was matter or "aurum vulgi" while Christ's blood was the redeeming "aurum philosophicum" ("Völsunga saga," ch. 29 & 31). The relationship between weaving and women's blood rituals comes through, it seems to me, in an account in *Njáls saga* ("Njal's Saga") of the battle at Clontarf between the Norse Vikings and King Brian Boru of Ireland. This historical event took place on Good Friday in 1014. The text depicts twelve Valkyries at the loom, weaving the bloody scene as it unfolds. At the time the battle raged in Dublin, a man is said to have gone outside his house at Caithness (County in NE-Scotland invaded by Norsemen) and he saw twelve persons riding up to a women's bower, and there they all disappeared from sight. He went up to the bower and looked through a window and saw that there were women in there with a loom set up before them. Men's heads were used in place of weights, and human entrails in place of the warp and woof; a sword served as the treadle and an arrow as the batten (ch. 157). As they weave their web, the women chant a poem describing the gory tableau as it takes shape on their loom. As if in a dream, they are simultaneously at the loom and in the heat of the battle. When the web was done the peeper saw them tear it down and into pieces, each holding on to what she had in her hands. He then walked away from the window and returned home but the women mounted their unsaddled steeds and rode six to the south and six to the north. Ultimately one would say that this goes back to the norns who wove the web of fate (although in *Völuspá* ["Prophecy of the Seeress"] they carved runes to determine men's fate, which implies that they invented writing). As I see it, the two poles of woman's cycle, ovulation with its life giving potential and menstruation

through the window of the tower in which she had her bower. "She sat by a golden runner onto which she embroidered my past deeds," the lovesick hero confides to Brynhild's nephew.[45] Brynhild's furious attempt to stand by her truth in the face of patriarchal oppression and deceit led to the hero's demise and her own suicide. For a young girl in the 18th century Icelandic countryside, the Valkyrie within would have been more than she could have embraced and integrated.

The Lunar Mirror

The lunar dimension is like a mirror that reflects our full potential. Hence its effect can be overpowering. Under normal circumstances, the unconscious does not confront us with content that we are not able to suffer and deal with. We may not want to face it, particularly if it runs counter to the ethical codes that have been imprinted on us, even if they impede our growth. But its emergence indicates that the moment is ripe and that something within us wants to get out into the light of day. What is called for is that we listen, wrestle with the images that the lunar mirror holds up to us, and integrate them. If we do not heed the call and cooperate, we suffer. This is certainly true of our protagonist.

We could argue that Thorunn squandered the magic moment, the

---

with its death and dissolution of that potential are reflected in the weaving and its being torn to pieces. Disruption of order was seemingly projected onto woman. She was the culprit. And so it was, according to the saga, King Brian's rancorous ex-wife, Queen Gormflaith, who instigated this bloody war. Here we are reminded of the conditions with which Odin returned Brísingamen to Freyja. Queen Gormflaith fits the formulaic prescription imposed on Freyja to perfection. The description of her in the saga is a memorable one: "the fairest of women and talented in matters over which she had no conscious control, but it is said," the story repeats, "that she was badly gifted where her will was brought to bear" (ch. 154). But then, at its core, *Njáls saga* is about the transition from heathendom to Christianity. The Valkyries were part of the old order which drowned in a blood bath of their making, on Good Friday of all days, while the slain king Brian's Christian blood instantly became a miraculous healing source.

45   "Völsunga saga," ch. 24.

kairos, as experienced by Thorn-Rose's prince when the blossoming thornhedge opened up to him. That would have been a thorn stuck in her soul. But then Thorunn lived in the real world and not in a fairy tale, and it was a world excessively hostile to feminine nature. We understand her fear. For her to accept the guidance of the "hidden woman" would have required a heroic approach, not that of a warrior charging forth against an enemy with a brandished sword, but that of a surrender to her feminine nature and acceptance of its creative, healing, and enriching insights.

Thorunn's encounter with the "hidden woman" captured the minds of people three centuries ago. That it is being wrestled with here suggests that the issue it raises has not been resolved. We remember the princes who through generations had tried to break through the thornhedge surrounding Thorn-Rose but did not succeed until someone with a new approach appeared on the scene. Thorunn's reality may appear to have little in common with ours, but if in fact the tale is about her initiation, as I believe it is, we seem to still buy into the negative propaganda towards menstruation. It pervades our culture and hence may be accepted uncritically, without questioning. By taking a close and informed look at our foremothers' experiences, we might become inspired to approach female menstrual power in a new and more creative way. It might motivate us to replace our negative attitude with reverence for its magnitude and to trust in the guidance of the woman in the cave.

To sum it up, what would we say was the cause of Thorunn's misfortune? Her looking back? The "hidden woman's" evil eye? Thorunn's flight from her nature and denial of her power? Or was it the misguided indoctrination of her culture? Whatever the answer, it seems fair to conclude that the enmity Thorunn projected on the blue-clad woman brought withering on her budding womanhood. Then we can speculate whether this dismal conclusion was a projection by the spirit of her time on the maiden's loss of innocence.

5
Katla's Dream

from *Icelandic Folk and Fairy Tales*, I &VI

collected by Jón Árnason

This is my retelling of the poem "Katla's Dream" in volume VI of the collection with some amplifications and an addition at the end from the prose version of the story in volume I. The poet's voice comes through as he or she revives people and events from a distant past.

Már was the noblest chieftain who lived at Reykjanes. I believe his wife's name was Katla. She came from an important family. It is said that they loved each other dearly, were a good match, and never had a quarrel during their entire conjugal life.

One day Már rode to Althing with a flock of valorous men. He left Katla behind and told her to sew him a shirt. One morning, in beautiful weather, Katla went to her bower to carry out her task, but no sooner had she sat down than she fell asleep. Other women came to the bower but Katla continued to sleep, undisturbed. Close to noon they tried to awaken her, but there was no way they could. They feared that she was dead and told her foster-father. When he came to where she sat, he found breath stirring in her chest, but he could not awaken her. Mournful, he sat by her for full four days. On the fifth day it is said that Katla woke up and was visibly sad but nobody dared inquire about the reason for her sorrow.

When Már arrived home from Althing he found Katla's demeanor changed, for neither did she come out to welcome him nor did she bow to him when he came. This had never happened before. Már asked his wife who had caused this change in her. He assured her that she would not come to harm for telling him the reason for her sorrow. Katla said that she would disclose her grievances to him though she kept them secret from others, for she knew that due to his love and other virtues he would prove to be her best support.

"I felt," she said, "that a woman came to me in the bower. She had the proud bearing of a mistress. Her words unfolded like growing herbs and sounded pleasing to my ears. She called me 'her Katla' and asked me to go out with her. She said that her spirits would guard my seat so that nobody would be alarmed. We walked away from your farm till we came to a river. There I saw a richly equipped ferry. I then decided to ask her name. She told me that I could call her Alvör and said that grief had compelled her to come see me. No sooner did she lift me on board the ferry than I lost command of my will. Alvör plied the oars, and the ferry found its way across the rapid stream. I saw a small house by the foaming river. It turned out to be her home. She then laid hands on me, and I forgot my ardent love for you.

"She led me into a splendidly furnished hall where elegant ladies were seated, all of whom acted as if they knew me. Then Alvör quietly touched a man whom she called Kári and asked him to awaken. 'I have news for you,' she said to him. 'Katla is here in the hall.' The well-mannered, silk-clad man awoke and wished health and good fortune on me for having come to see him, although he himself would come to suffer grief. He called me a dutiful and virtuous woman and said that I had awakened him, 'that is a gift your love has brought me,' he said, 'but I will die when you walk away from here.'

"Alvör had a tub-bath prepared for me. She then lifted a cup of wine to my lips before I lay down with her son Kári. She said that disaster would befall me if I refused my love to him who had been in the throes of perilous sorrow for a long time. Her will had to prevail for I was no longer in possession of my senses, and so it was the whole time I was away from your farm.

"One morning Alvör came to the bed in which we slept together and said that I would have to get dressed though it would cause grief to her son. Kári moaned aloud and held me tight to his chest when I rose to leave his bed, and I myself would have desired to be there longer had fate not parted us. He told me that we would have a son. 'Name him Kári,' he said, and added that we would never see each other again during our lifetime on this earth. He gave me a belt, a knife, and a ring which I was to keep for our son so that he would remember his father when he came of age. 'But to you,' said Kári, 'I give a mantle of pure gold, a necklace, and a buckle, all of which will be considered treasures by those who lay eyes on them. I bid you own these till old age.' Unwilling, I had to stand up and put on all my finery, I could linger no longer. Then Alvör came and sternly took both my hands. She led me to the ferry by which we came before, seized the oars and set out across the river again. She escorted me to the house and fetched back her guardian spirits. Nobody knew about my disappearance from the farm nor when I would come back. She exhorted me to hide my sorrows till the end of winter by which time they will become manifested and told me to lay the blame on her when word gets out."

Winter passed, and shortly before summer, Katla gave birth to a son with beautiful eyes. Már was devoted to the boy, but his mother was more remote. Már had him named Kári, for he did not want to swerve from what the mother had secretly disclosed to him. Half a year went by and Katla became pregnant again and gave birth to another son. Now she wanted to pick the name and declared that he should be called Ari. The boys grew up together and Már loved them both equally, but to his grief Katla was cool and indifferent towards Kári. "Why do you bear these grudges towards your son, Katla?" he asked. "It hurts me deeply that you hate the child and yet you know my feelings for him." "You are an admirably virtuous man, Már, to be so loving and faithful to someone unrelated to you," she said. "That is why I ask you to never let the young boy suffer on my account." "I promise to love your son as if he were begotten by me," Már readily responded.

Time passed and, as far as everyone knew, harmonious love reigned between Katla and Már. The boys grew up for five or six years, and nothing worth reporting happened. Then one morning Már went to work with his farmhands at an early hour because apparently the weather was calm and favorable for fishing. Katla remained blissfully asleep in their conjugal bed when an imposing Alvör came to her bedside. "How very different is our situation, Katla. You live in happiness with your husband, but I grieve my deceased son and get no amends for this bale. That is why you shall have to make this choice, which no doubt you will find difficult, either to lose Már at sea today or suffer that your son disgrace you by his words." Faced with such oppressive options, Katla responded tearfully: "I leave the curses to fate, but to lose Már is the last thing I want." At that they left their discussion, both with a grieving heart.

When Már came home in the evening he saw that Katla was distressed and asked who had upset her. "Alvör came to cheer me up again," she replied mournfully and told him the whole story. Már responded with valor and told her to let go of her worries. He assured her that he would find a way out of these difficulties and that he would keep all his promises to her. "Let us prepare a feast and invite your brothers," he said. "Your honor will be restored and you shall not take their words to heart. Be cheerful towards all and do not speak till your turn comes."

Már rode with many men to welcome the brothers, all of whom were important chieftains. The brothers were appreciative of their sister's graceful reception. They were shown to the seats of honor and wine was generously served. Katla wore the mantle that Kári gave to her, and her necklace was praised as a treasure by all. Then Már addressed the guests and asked that a truce be honored by all who drank at his table. The brothers agreed and emphasized that whoever broke the truce would pay amends. The wine made them merry and cordial toward each other. When Katla had taken her seat and the boys were playing on the floor, Kári asked his mother to lend him her necklace, and so she did. When Ari saw this, he became jealous that his mother indulged his brother more than him. "Give me that gold ring, I want to play with it," he demanded. Kári declined. "You refuse to give it to me, you son of a whore! Our possessions belong to me alone!"

The guests listened in wonder to the boys' squabble but Katla left her seat, tormented again by the old remorse. She went to bed with a bursting heart and said that she would rather die than her sorrow be known. But while she mourned in bed, there was no calm where her brothers sat. They picked up on the boy's words, infuriated that their sister had called shame on their family. They vowed to avenge by the sword, for surely she had been disgraced by someone. The child did not know how to lie, they claimed, therefore there had to be some truth in his words. Már then said valiantly:

"Listen noblemen, it is absurd to take seriously the words children happen to know and speak." The proud brothers raged at his words, and there was no assuaging their anger. They were determined, they said, to find the reason behind the boys' dispute and accused Már and Katla of having cunningly hidden a crime of which the boys had gotten a whiff.

"Listen to me, chieftains," Már then said. "I have never reproached Katla nor wanted her tainted in any way. But tell me, virtuous noblemen, how can someone who falls into disgrace unwillingly or experiences illusions in sleep be held responsible?" He left the hall in distress and went to see Katla, who could barely speak from grief. "In order to remedy your misfortune, take my advice and tell your brothers the whole story or else we will have a bloody battle on our hands," he said. Although she found it difficult to reveal her sorrows and would much prefer death, with a heavy heart she went to her four brothers who received her coolly for hatred was in their minds. "Tell them your story, Katla," Már encouraged her, "maybe it will ease their minds and abate their compulsion for revenge." Katla then told them her story from beginning to end. As they listened, they became deeply affected by her plight and concluded that she was innocent of her misfortunes. To Már the brothers said: "You are a wise and noble man. You have kept Katla's woe from becoming public, and for that you will have our lifelong friendship."

Már and Katla stayed in love till old age took them to the grave. Ari, son of Már, became an important chieftain and took after his father in most things. He had great many descendants as can be read in old books of knowledge. As to Kári, I have heard that Már had him fostered up in Rennidalur, arranged a good marriage for him and gave him generously of his riches. He became a well-to-do farmer and was held to possess hidden knowledge. Yet he was well liked. He knew the laws of tides and the art of astrology.

Some say that Kári, son of Kári, often went to see his grandmother when he was growing up and learned from her wisdom that "hidden people" practiced in the days of old. It therefore did not serve people well to wrong him. But then few would be inclined to do so, for he was well liked and held in regard by those in authority. When Már had passed away, it is said that Kári took both his mother Katla and his grandmother Alvör under his roof. They however did not get along and Kári frequently had to reconcile them. Once he came upon them in the midst of a quarrel and it is said that he lost his temper, which he was not wont to do. When he had stood there a little while, fire flared up through the floor, and his grandmother Alvör burned to ashes on the spot. Whether Kári caused the burning of his grandmother or whether the fire was ignited by the fanaticism of the old hag is not clear. Yet it has been rumored that Kári killed his grandmother.

It is further told that after Alvör had come twice to chagrin Katla as is said before, the latter had the entrance at Reykhólar turned towards the mountain, as it does to this day, contrary to the other farms in the region. This she did in order not to have to see Alvör's house, which supposedly was visible from her door while it faced south, and thereby have her sorrows re-awakened. It is also said that she did not want to go to the Reykhólar-pool, which is located south of the farm, because she felt too close to Alvör's home. Instead, she went a good distance from the farm and bathed in a pool that stands apart and is known to this day as Katla's Pool.

INTERPRETATION

The Vessel and the Wind

"The artist hits the nail thoroughly on the head when she shows civilization grow out of woman's womb," says one male critique about the work of Ishrat Jahan in the exhibit *Women of the World*.[1] Jahan, who is from Bangladesh, states that the theme of her painting is "that civilization flourishes from the womb of a woman, but the world is burdened by civilization and has become sick."[2] "Katla's Dream" engendered by the psyche of the Icelandic people at the time of a religious transition, exemplifies the civilizing role of woman. Katla's name is derived from *ketill* which means "cauldron." Óðrerir, the vessel that contained the mead of poetry was referred to as *ketill* (see Page 83). *Kári*, the name of Katla's otherworldly lover, means "wind." Katla's function in the story suggests that she personifies the womb as a transforming vessel, where the old dissolves to be reborn in a new form that suits a new time. The Icelandic folk tale, believed to have originated a thousand years ago, and the modern artwork from Bangladesh are rooted in a collective reality, which is independent of time and space. Both impart an invaluable lesson to us who inhabit the modern world of technology and are in danger of losing touch with our roots.

The story as it appears in this collection is my retelling of the poem "Katla's Dream," with the addition at the end of a short passage from the prose version of the story. The poem is believed to be based on lost material, and some have deduced that its roots reach back to

1 Bjarnason in *Morgunbladid*, April 5th 2004.

2 *Women of the World: A Global Collection of Art*, p. 29.

the period of transition from heathendom to Christianity (around 1000). It is believed to have been composed sometime during the last centuries before the conversion from Catholicism to Lutheranism (1550), when the Church fought with increasing ardor against the studies of ancient knowledge and folk tales. The prose version of the tale is believed to be derived from the poem. When we read "Katla's Dream," therefore we need to keep in mind the cultural situation in both the 10th and the 15th centuries. In the 10th century practicing *seiðr*, which involved ecstatic communion with the otherworld, had become a crime that was severely punished by law. Women who so did were most often stoned to death and sometimes sources mention burnings at the stake.[3] This goes hand-in-hand with the Bible's prohibition of "wicked customs" into which category *seiðr* would have fallen. In Katla's story, we detect both a dialogue with Christian doctrine as well as an attempt to counterbalance the one-sidedness of the Church which strove to suppress the ancient heritage. We also see a transition from the retributive mindset that marked the old world to the ideal of love and forgiveness. In fact, Love is at the heart of the tale. It is the optimal good, and it is Alvör, Katla's dream self, who is instrumental in bringing it forth and ensuring its integration into the culture. When Alvör challenges Katla to choose between Már and her own reputation, it is a matter of his life or hers. Katla risks her life for the love of her husband, as does Már risk his life for his love of her by standing firmly by her in the face of an impossible situation. But what may be particularly instructive to us, the offspring, is the cultural attitude revealed in the tale toward women and feminine nature, an inheritance that we embody and need to be aware of.

The opening of the tale leaves us in no doubt that Már is the principal character in this drama. Its basic theme revolves around the redeeming influence Katla's dream has on the male dominated

---

3   Árnason, II, pp. xvii- xviii.

society. We do not see any comparable transformation in Katla herself. Quite the contrary, her dream throws her into conflict with herself. The tale, I think it is safe to say, does not leave us with a satisfying resolution to Katla's predicament. It is left to subsequent generations of women to find a constructive solution to the dilemma. Katla's "big dream" is an archetypal and thus, a timeless experience that is charged with energy which may still work its magic if approached with an open mind.

Kári, whom Alvör asks be called "bridegroom" in the prose version, is by virtue of his name a personification of the invisible and unruly "wind." He is a "hidden man" kin to Freyja's husband Od, a wild (uncivilized) spirit even if his demeanor is that of a courtier. Thus, the symbolic names of the protagonists indicate that they represent certain powers and values. But even so, the tale conveys their feelings with sensitivity, regardless of whether they belong to this world or the one beyond. "Grief" compelled Alvör to ravish Katla into the "hidden world," and necessity drives her to subject Katla to two impossible choices, for otherwise her experience would not have affected the collective and brought about the needed transformation. On that occasion, both women left the discussion with a "grieving heart." Alvör's sorrow accords with Jung's statement "that our unconscious is an acting and suffering subject with an inner drama" and hence in some real way an independent being.[4] As far as Katla is concerned, we experience her as a person of flesh and blood, but above all, she represents the feminine and women of her time.

Duties of Married Couples according to St. Paul

At the outset, harmony and a clear division of duties characterize the conjugal life at Reykhólar. Katla serves Már with the needle–he

---

4   Vol. 9: 1, par. 8.

tells her to sew him a shirt while he rides off to Althing, and when she does not show him due deference upon arrival–she did not "bow to him" as she was wont to do, he realizes that everything is not as it ought to be. On close inspection, it is as if St. Paul's prescription of duties to married couples forms the warp into which the tale of Katla and Már is woven:

> Wives, submit to your own husbands, as to the Lord. For the husband is head of the wife, as also Christ is the head of the church; and he is the Saviour of the body. Therefore, just as the church is subject to Christ, so *let* the wives *be* to their own husbands in everything.[5]

The body of the wife is likened to the church, and this temple is under the lordship of the husband and his path toward God. As Eve was made from Adam's rib, so the church is considered to be born from the wound in Christ's side, and in like manner, Már projects his inner woman, or *anima* (Lat. for "soul") as Jung called the male's feminine counterpart, onto Katla. To this image she shall conform. Her story reveals how woman becomes the means through which the male perfects himself by cleansing her:

> Husbands, love your wives, just as Christ also loved the church and gave himself for it, that he might sanctify and cleanse it with the washing of water by the word.[6]

While Katla's brothers react to their sister's defilement by reaching for the sword, Már brandishes the sword figuratively by applying reason and thereby cleanses her in their eyes by his words. As Christ loved the church and gave himself for it, so Már gave himself for Katla though standing by her could have cost him his life. In like manner, he becomes her savior for had it not been for him, the male dominated society presented by her chieftain brothers would have made her pay dearly. Death seems to have been

---

5   Eph. 5:22-24.

6   Ibid. 5:25-26.

the expected penalty, for she would rather die than reveal her sin, even if it might save her. *Már* is a bird's name and means "seagull." Már's mental prowess and oversight are thus emphasized, qualities inherited by his son *Ari*, whose name means "eagle." In contrast, Katla's earthiness is brought to the fore by the natural pool that is named for her and in which she bathes.

St. Paul points the way toward original oneness through love and specific role playing in the married couple:

> *"For this reason a man shall leave his father and mother and be joined to his wife, and the two shall become one flesh."* This is a great mystery, but I speak concerning Christ and the church. Nevertheless let each one of you in particular so love his own wife as himself, and let the wife *see* that she respects *her* husband.[7]

As Adam and Eve were one flesh at the outset, so Katla and Kári are "one flesh," for Kári is Katla's *animus* (Latin for "spirit") as Jung called the woman's masculine counterpart or inner man. St. Paul prescribes that this inner reality is to be transferred onto the human partner. The tale however reveals "betrayal" of this contract to be a precondition for human progress. Katla's blissful union with Kári engenders a social transformation towards love and benevolence. But Katla feels that she has committed adultery and experiences herself as a sinner. St. Paul follows his exhortation to husbands to "love their own wives as their own bodies" with words that are descriptive of Már's attitude toward Katla but read like irony when applied to her: "for no one ever hated his own flesh, but nourishes and cherishes it, just as the Lord *does* the church."[8] Katla "hates" her son Kári who is flesh of her flesh, and she goes to extremes to avoid Alvör, who personifies feminine nature. The emphasis on the pool that bears her name, and with which her story closes, implies her need for purification and may hint at the menstrual theme that

---

7 Ibid. 5:31-33.

8 Ibid. 5:28-29.

seems to underlie her experience. She lavishes declarations of love and admiration on Már for his virtues, but we do not get the feeling that Katla loves and cherishes herself.

Intervention of a Higher Consciousness

The story is set in motion when Már rides off to Althing, which is the domain of Wordly law, but Katla goes to her bower and tours her inner dimensions where Nature reigns. Alvör invades her consciousness in an effort to establish balance in a one-sided world, which is governed by the might of the sword and in danger of splitting away from its heritage and natural origin. Alvör incarnates law on the subjective level. She makes sure that Katla does not overstay her welcome in the otherworld. She is allowed four days, the same number of days as Freyja stayed in the stone with the four dwarfs, from whom she obtained her legendary Brísingamen. Four being "the number of order in the universe," Alvör's vigilance points to an organizing principle in the unconscious.[9]

Alvör is the "all-seeing."[10] Katla experiences her as an authoritative figure. She describes her bearing as that of a lady–the term she uses is *húsfreyja*, "lady of the house," and her words like the "unfolding of growing herbs" point to a goddess of the earth, a mother figure from whom Katla has become estranged. The paradox in Katla's description is that she is herself a *húsfreyja*, but in comparison with Alvör's power, her status is slight. Alvör is the image in the mirror, Katla's higher self who attempts to shake her out of passivity and steer her toward emancipation. By confronting Katla with two inordinately difficult choices, Alvör brings her free will to the fore.

---

9   http://www.britannica.com/EBchecked/topic/1086324/the-number-four

10   The latter part of Alvör's name -vör refers to being "vigilant," related to Germ. *wer-, IE. *ụer- "sense, observe, see." The prefix al- is the same as "all," emphasizing the absoluteness of the faculty in question.

Magic Circle

The poem is studded with metaphors. Thus the rapid river across which Alvör ferrys Katla is called "blood of the earth." A common denominator for Katla and Alvör is the poetic circumlocution *seima Gerd*.[11]

Seima is gen. pl. of *seimir*, an obsolete word for "serpent" and related to *seimur* which means "a thread of gold."[12] In the last chapter, we explored the serpent's relationship with the oracular priestesses and the Earth-Mother of whom it was born and how the ancients regarded it as a knower of all the secrets hidden in the earth. This trait is reflected in *Alvör's* name as defined above. "She called me 'her Katla,'" Katla says when she describes her encounter with Alvör to her husband. It is an address that betrays intimacy between mother and daughter and hints at a maternal legacy from which Katla has become alienated, namely that she is the carrier of the vessel, the *ketill*, that contains the precious mead of poetry. We also saw the snake's kinship with the uterus, both of which renew themselves by shedding the old skin. The latter meaning, *seimur* as "thread of gold," evokes the Spinster who spins the thread of life and befits Alvör's role in the tale as she prevents the collective from breaking with its past. The thread that connects Alvör and Katla, who stands in essence for every woman's reality, is the golden path of evolution that leads from the primal source to the fulfillment of human potential.

Gerd (a name related to *gerdi* = "hedge") is "she who is enclosed."[13] In the interpretation of Thorn-Rose, who is enclosed by a thornhedge,

---

11   A circumlocution of this sort is called *kenning* in Old Norse and Icelandic poetry.

12   The word *seimur* also refers to "honey cake; honeycomb," in which case it is traced to OHG and MHG *seim, seime*= "muscous membrane, viscid liquid," and Gr. *(h)aima* "blood," derived from IE *sei* = "drip, flow" (Magnússon). There exist numerous myths about serpents being fed honey cakes. For instance in The Anonymous "Nature Worship and Mystical Series" attributed to Rev. Hargrave Jennings (1817-1890), Herodotus is quoted as saying that "in the Acropolis at Athens was kept a serpent who was considered the guardian of the city. He was fed on cakes of honey once a month" (http://www.sacred-texts.com/etc/wos/wos06.htm.).

13   Motz, p. 124.

I touched on the serpent who bites its tail and girdles the virginal bower. This is a microcosmic reflection of the ouroboros Midgard Serpent who encircles the earth in Norse mythology. Although not girdled by a venomous serpent, Katla is protected for four days by a magic circle of sorts that the household does not manage to break. Within this space, time and eternity, the secular and the sacred, merge and sow something new in consciousness. It seems legitimate to deduce that *seima Gerd* is a euphemism for a menstruating woman, rooted in the memory of women's inviolate seclusion during their period.

Gerd is the heroine of *Skírnismál* ("Lay of Skírnir"), one of the poems in the *Elder Edda*. By virtue of her generic name, Gerd is an archetype. She is encircled by a wall of fire in the giant world–and by a wooden fence to boot, with two ferocious dogs[14] guarding the gate— when Skírnir, messenger of the fertility god and Freyja's twin, Freyr, rides through the roaring flames and forces Gerd to give herself in marriage to the god.[15] The poem imparts a dark and cruel picture of how women's voluntary seclusion was turned into its opposite. Gerd is on the way to her bower when she is spotted by Freyr, who had sat himself on Odin's throne from which all worlds could be observed. The god's description of Gerd is that of the sun. Her shining arms lighten up the heaven and the sea. His desire for her drives him into depression, which prompts his servant, Skírnir, to go on a wooing journey to the giants' world on his master's behalf, equipped with the latter's sword.

---

14   We are reminded of the hounds of the Roman goddess Diana, who presided over women's mysteries.

15   I understand the name *Skírnir* to mean "he who purifies." It has been explained as "the bright one," derived from adj. *skír* = "bright, pure." But as Skírnir is an agent in this myth who attempts to convert the autonomous giant maiden from her loyalty to a worldview that antedates that of Odin, to whose pantheon Freyr had come to belong, it seems to me more logical that he be connected with the verb *skíra* = "cleanse, baptize" (Magnússon, p. 846). I use the word *convert* for Skírnir's proceedings bear an uncanny resemblance to those of the Frankish and Norse missionary kings who christianized the reluctant populace by the sword (*Saga Íslands*, I, pp. 227-228). What seems to be at the core of this poem, obscure to the modern mind, is a deep-seated conflict between different religious worldviews.

Gerd is portrayed as a strong and independent woman who stands up proudly to Skírnir. He tries in vain to bribe her with precious gifts, then showers her with threats and intimidations. When she turns a deaf ear to his threat to cut off her head, he strikes her with a "taming wand" and declares that he will tame her through sorcery. He then paints a grim picture of what awaits her in the giants' world which she is so reluctant to leave.[16] It will become a hell where she will be oppressed by evil spirits and endure pain and distress in cohabitation with a three-headed *thurs*. He recites a litany of magical characters intended to adversely affect her flow of *tears*. Yet again, we seem to encounter a reference to Freyja's tear of red-gold, which we have come to associate with menstrual blood. With great fanfare, calling on giants, *thurses* and gods, Skírnir issues a ban intended to prevent Gerd from enjoying a man. When he finally threatens to carve her the *thurs*-rune, her resistance breaks (see Page 28). This is the turning point. Gerd not only relinquishes her sovereignty but also her "rimed chalice, filled with ancient mead," an attribute that linked her with Lady Sovereignty[17]. Her response to Skírnir at this point sounds like an echo of Christ's appeal to God in the garden of Gethsemane: "Take this cup from me!" Freyr's victory over the giant maiden is confirmed in "Ynglinga saga" by Snorri Sturluson where Freyr is titled lord over the Swedes (*freyr* means "lord"). His wife was Gerd and they had a son named Fjölnir. The nightmarish

---

16   The description of "The Seclusion of Girls at Puberty" in Frazer's *The Golden Bough* opened my eyes to what lies behind the cruel picture Skírnir paints for Gerd and made me realize that it is not merely a distorted fantasy but a reality which at one time or another has been inflicted on women. With such memories from the past imprinted in their bodies, we need not be surprised at women's negative attitude toward menstruation. While the details of Skírnir's threats and Frazer's account lie outside the scope of my interpretation, it is nonetheless worth citing the latter's explanation for the widespread seclusion of pubescent girls, namely "the deeply engrained dread which primitive man universally entertains of menstruous blood. He fears it at all times but especially on its first appearance; hence the restrictions under which women lie at their first menstruation are usually more stringent than those which they have to observe at any subsequent recurrence of the mysterious flow" (p. 698).

17   St. 37; see also notes 7 & 8 in Chapter 4.

world Skírnir describes to Gerd is quite different from that of Alvör in Katla's dream which might be seen as a compensation for the negative picture impressed upon women by patriarchal culture.

Within the protecting circle cast around Katla, linear time and the timeless intersect. Menstruation links woman back to the original wellspring from which culture unfolds. It is as if during this time a passage opens up between the two separate hemispheres of the brain, as if Katla's crossing over takes her out of the left hemisphere, which is under the dominion of her husband and the male oriented culture. It is from "his" farm, she repeatedly emphasizes, that Alvör leads her and ferries her over into the other sphere, the land beyond where time is non-existent and unity reigns.

In *My Stroke of Insight* neuroanatomist Jill Bolte Taylor, who through a stroke lost the function of her left brain, describes her experience of being caught in the silence of the right hemisphere where image is the mode of expression and where she felt at one with all the energy that is. In this mode of being the notion of "we" prevails as opposed to the "I" of the isolated individual who is ruled by the left hemisphere. Dr. Taylor describes this dimension of interconnectedness as the land of peace and euphoria, a Nirvana. And she claims that we can purposefully choose "to step to the right of our left hemisphere." By so doing we will contribute to making our world more peaceful. This becomes, in fact, the consequence of Katla's crossing over. The male oriented society evolves toward more peaceful ways while war rages within Katla herself.

ACE OF CUPS

The Cup and the Necklace

Katla's union with Kári is initiated by Alvör's ministering wine to her. She loses all will of her own in her interaction with the otherworldly powers and returns pregnant from her journey into the "hidden" dimension.

In tarot, the Cup is a symbol of love, feelings and emotions, of dreams and creative imagination, of healing. It is a uniting symbol in contrast to the sword that sunders. In the Ace of Cups from the Rider-Waite-Smith version (see image), we see a white dove bringing from above a white circular wafer with an even-handed cross on it and dropping it into a golden overflowing chalice. This is an image of the Eucharist, but the symbolism behind it goes far beyond Christianity. Echoing the unifying concept of the Cup, "the cross in a circle is an astrological symbol for Earth and a synthesis of Christianity and Pagan tradition."[18] The white dove, symbol of the Holy Spirit and bringer of peace, was an attribute of Aphrodite, goddess of Love. Thus we see reflected in the Ace of Cups, *"container of primal energy,"* the essence of the mission bestowed on Katla through her dream. We have already seen, that by virtue of her name, *Katla* is that container of transforming energy. She is a vehicle for a higher intelligence to bring about reform in a cruel world of unbridled feuds. The tenor of the tale, however, confirms that woman was, somewhere along the road, robbed of the gifts inherent in her feminine nature. Far from rejoicing in her cornucopia, Katla experiences herself as a sinful victim rather than a co-creator.

Katla's intercourse with Kári, her dream bridegroom, has all the characteristics of a "sacred marriage." The necklace (also referred to as a gold ring) that Kári bestows on her, is of particular importance in this context and refers back to Freyja's Brísingamen, which we have explored at length in previous chapters. The mantel of pure gold

---

18   *The Tarot School Correspondence Course*. Lesson 4, p. 11.

which he presents to her, puts Katla in the role of the sun while Kári, "the wind," embodies the invisible spirit. He is an anthropomorphic image of the dove as Holy Ghost who drops the wafer into the gold cup on the tarot card. It could be said that in Katla's dream Kári restores the feminine to its original splendor, but Katla is unable to embrace and integrate her imperial power.

To emphasize what has been said before, Freyja's cognomen was *Bride of the Vanir*. The Vanir were a family of gods worshipped by our agricultural ancestors. An important aspect of the Vanir-worship was *seiðr*, a ritual that consisted in reconnecting with the divine origin through ecstasy. We see this ancient custom play out in Katla's dream. Freyja was a Vanir-goddess, and it was she who introduced the art of *seiðr* to Odin and his pantheon of Æsir who arrived later on the stage of human evolution. As *seiðr* was based on surrender rather than conquest, it was considered the province of females in the Æsir-religion. Males who practiced *seiðr* were stigmatized as homosexuals and non-heroic. It did not deter Odin from engaging in the practice. From Snorri's description in *Heimskringla*, we can conclude that he had no qualms using it to his own ends, for not only did it enable him to know the fate of men and future events, but also to inflict death, misfortune, or illness, as well as to take reason or power from men and give to others.[19]

Seiðr is Dionysian in nature. As defined by Jungian analyst George R. Elder, Dionysus was "the deity of ecstasy caused by drinking wine or of any ecstatic experience, of sex or emotional religion."[20] We see Katla's experience mirrored in this description. Her precognitive gifts come through in that her dreams translate into reality. This is particularly clear in the latter dream where she foresees that her son will slander her. The tale gives an insight into the healing aspect

---

19   "Ynglinga saga," ch. 7.

20   P. 334.

of the *seiðr* as Katla's journey into another dimension brings about healing in the masculine. At the same time, it reveals the animosity of the ruling mindset toward the *völva* and the *seiðr*.

Muse and Mother

"Poet I am not, but the 'hidden woman' calls me," sings one of Iceland's best loved poets Jónas Hallgrímsson (1807-1845). Though sex does not figure in this inspiring encounter, the poet addresses the "hidden woman" as a lover whose kiss he desires, proving yet again that creation is an erotic affair between the conscious mind and the unconscious. As the "hidden woman" calls the poet, so Od calls Freyja who searches for him amongst foreign peoples. Nature is indeed the muse of the rational mind, but our culture has cast woman in the former role and the male in that of the rational mind. This role casting is particularly evident in Katla's story.

Jungian analyst Erich Neumann speculates whether woman's natural tendency to concretize instead of realizing may count for the "smallness of her spiritual achievements" as compared with those of men. He says:

> Instead of realizing, she concretizes, and, by a natural pro-jection, transposes the creative process of pregnancy onto the external plane. That is to say, woman takes the sym-bols of this phase of matriarchal consciousness literally; she loves, becomes pregnant, bears, nourishes, cherishes, and so on, and lives her femininity outwardly but not in the inner world. This tendency may explain the smallness of her spiritual achievements as compared to men, her lack of creative productivity. It seems to a woman (rightly or wrongly?) that the source of life in pregnancy and birth is creative enough.[21]

Katla would seem to prove his point. She takes her impregnation

---

21   1954, p. 98.

by her dream lover literally and invests the potential held up to her by her dream in her biological son. Or rather, her culture does, for her dream stands apart from the rest of the tale. The cultural situation called for a mediator between the old heritage in danger of being lost and new times, which would not have welcomed in a woman the qualities attributed to the son, Kári. This is borne out by the fate of Alvör who is burnt to ashes. What Neumann does not take into account in his assessment of woman's spiritual achievements is the active suppression of women's spiritual, artistic, and cultural possibilities.

On her road to emancipation and freedom, woman has colluded with patriarchy's mindset and repressive attitude toward her own nature as is exemplified by Katla. On the rare occasions that Katla asserts herself, she sides with the masculine. Her decision to name her son Ari stands out in the poem and points to her deference for her husband's mental agility, and her architectural maneuverings in order not to be reminded of Alvör and her past grievances show a firm intention to oust her feminine power and wisdom. The ethics of the times compelled her to choose between creative exploration of her inner world and her conjugal commitment. She could not have both.

The *völva* transmitted her visions to her community. The message Katla brings to the outer world is invested in Kári's gifts, which she is told to show. In the tale, they are concretized rather than read as symbols, the wisdom of which a dreamer should integrate and translate into reality. But Katla's dream is not of a personal nature. It concerns the community, as is the hallmark of a *völva*. The belt intended for the son differentiates as well as unites the lower, instinctual part of the body and the upper regions of the mind and feelings. It symbolizes the middle way between heaven and earth embodied by Kári the son and his knowledge of the stars and the tides and currents of the sea. The knife differentiates one thing from another, which is a prerequisite for seeing things for what they are. The ring on the other hand is a uniting symbol and denotes eternal cyclicity, which in a nutshell is reflected in the moon and the menstrual cycle. The mantle of pure gold that Kári gives to her, the necklace – *men* – and the clasp, a uniting symbol, refer to the sacred marriage as symbolized by the conjunction of the sun and the moon. But Katla does not feel like a radiating sun when she arises from her bridal bed with Kári. She does not awaken to a renewed consciousness infused with energy. She is sadness incarnated, torn by guilt for having surrendered to her dream husband.

Animus

In *The Grail Legend* by Emma Jung, we find this interesting observation which reveals the universality of Katla's dream content:

> In the dreams and fantasies of even happily married women, a mysteriously fascinating masculine figure often appears, a demonic or divine dream or shadow lover to which Jung has given the name of *animus*. Not uncommonly, the woman cherishes a more or less conscious secret idea that one of her children, preferably the oldest or youngest, was fathered by this psychic lover. Superhuman powers will readily be attributed to such a child.[22]

It is common knowledge that many a mother desires to see her dreams realized by her offspring instead of cultivating what is called for in herself. Our tale certainly endows Kári with supernatural powers, but as far as Katla is concerned the analogy ends there. She does not live through her son as those ambitious mothers do. She shows aversion for Alvör's legacy and projects it out, as if purging herself, onto her son.

The son begotten in Katla's dream is her psychological child, her awakening masculinity, which, if consciously cultivated, would

---

22   P. 46.

enable her to carry her heritage forth in a wise and balanced manner. Marie-Louise von Franz addresses the necessity for woman to develop her *animus*. She says: "On [the] highest level the inner man acts as a bridge to the Self. He personifies a woman's capacities of courage, spirit and truth and connects her to the source of her personal creativity."[23] Here we need to be aware that we are talking about qualities that the culture has attributed to the male and hence defined as masculine. "Katla's Dream" is a reminder of how the culturally defined gender roles have thwarted woman's progress.

When Katla sits down with the needle at the beginning of the tale, it is because her husband has commanded her to sew him a shirt. In like manner, she puts her trust in him to think and act for her. On the rare occasions that she takes an initiative, her actions are turned against her nature and distance her from her nurturing roots. Von Franz points out that "to transform the animus involves immense suffering for it means nothing less than forsaking an old identity for a new one." Looking at the tale from this point of view, it is indeed true that the transformation that takes place on the collective level costs pain and suffering for Katla and her part personalities, Alvör and Kári. From von Franz's statement it could be inferred that, in accordance with the demands of the times, woman, personified by Katla, forsakes her old identity as *völva* for that of a wife who devotes herself wholly and completely to her husband as if he were the Lord. Katla's suffering was not for naught, though, for it brought about more humane social conditions under the auspices of Love. From that perspective, Katla is a Christ figure who sacrifices an important part of herself for the good of all. But that very sacrifice prevents woman from developing her animus on her own premises. The prescription comes from outside of her. Her husband should be her Lord and spiritual guide.

---

23   1988, p. 215.

Von Franz does not mince her words when she talks about masculinity, or rather the lack of it, in women:

> A woman who has no animus has no pep, no enterprise, no intelligence, no initiative. She is a very poor creature. She is just a womb producing children and a hand cooking in the kitchen. A woman without an animus is nothing. So the animus is an exceedingly positive thing. It is intelligence. It is the spiritual longing. The whole spirituality of women is connected with the animus. So you can say that in a woman, the animus, her masculine side extends from Devil to Holy Ghost.[24]

It is instructive to contemplate Katla in the light of these words. When, in the prose version, Kári bursts from grief "with a loud crash," we hear a distant echo of Ymir's disintegration in the *Gap of Ginnungar*. It is towards her husband, who replaces her natural animus, that Katla's desire is now wholly devoted. A new order according to St. Paul comes into being.

In response to the church's repressive measures, the collective psyche comes up with a virgin birth that reaches back to its matriarchal roots. Katla brings a savior into a world that is splitting away from its heritage. The symbolic conception, left to the imagination in the Bible, is portrayed as an erotic act in the tale. The necessity of this interference from the chthonic powers is emphasized. At the same time, the tale makes it clear that intercourse with these powers is a finished chapter, not only for Katla, but for women in general. The torch has been passed on to the male.

As a farmer, the son Kári is heir to the agricultural worldview ruled by Freyja and the Vanir-gods. As a chieftain, the younger Ari would be a descendant of Odin and the garrulous Æsir-gods who arrived later on the scene and strove for supremacy. The mythological warfare between the two clans of gods comes through in the tension over Katla's necklace between the brothers. Freyja

---

24   Ibid., p. 285.

obtained Brísingamen from the chthonic powers. Odin had it stolen from her, but gave it back to her on the condition that she establish an eternal war between two kings. Now it so happens that Freyja's attribute, used previously by Odin in the service of war, becomes a vehicle towards reconciliation.

When Ari, a rising star of the ruling class, denounces his mother as a whore, we are reminded of the Christian missionary who slandered Freyja by calling her a bitch. Norse heritage betrays an aggressive intent to alienate woman from her natural animus who is cast either as Satan or a disgusting giant. In our tale, it is Alvör who is the bad influence. She had to be exterminated to prevent the story from repeating itself. But it is with Alvör as with Gullveig who was speared and burnt many times over in Valhalla, she lives still as every woman's potential.[25]

By ousting Alvör, Katla closes the door on her *völva* aspect. She thereby quenches her spiritual powers and deprives herself of the challenging adventure, which involves developing her animus on her own terms rather than following prescriptions and trusting in her husband to think for her. Katla has no roots in herself. Drifting like flotsam in both worlds, she has no independent will, no independent voice. She goes through an experience, which should affect her deeply, but she makes every effort to push it away, hammers on her love for Már, and sings endless praises to his virtues and kindness. Her guilt runs like a red thread through the story. On the surface it is clear that Katla feels that she has committed adultery. But can we help wondering whether, deep down, her suffering was not caused by the feeling of having betrayed herself?

---

25   *Völuspá* ("Prophecy of the Seeress"), st. 21.

6
The Witch's Ride

from *Icelandic folk and fairy tales, I*
collected by Jón Árnason

The storyteller's switching from the past to the present tense has been kept intact.

Once upon a time there was a pastor who was an esteemed and prosperous man. He was newly wed when these events took place. He had a young and charming wife whom he loved very much, a wife who also surpassed women in the neighboring provinces in skills and beauty. There was however one flaw in her conduct that greatly disturbed the pastor, namely that she disappeared every

Christmas night and nobody knew where she went. The pastor kept pressing her for an explanation, but she said that it was none of his concern. This was the only thing that came between them.

At some point a vagrant lad engaged himself into the pastor's services. He was puny and frail but was held to possess knowledge surpassing that of common folks. Now time passed and nothing worth reporting happened until Christmas. On Christmas Eve, the lad is in the stable combing and feeding the pastor's horses when, without notice, the pastor's wife enters and starts to chat with him about this and that. Suddenly she pulls a bridle from under her apron and puts it on the boy. Such is the magic power of the bridle that the lad suffers his mistress to mount him and immediately darts off like a bird in flight. He dashes over mountains and valleys, rocks and boulders, and whatever else comes in his way; he is under the impression that he wades through heavy smoke. At last they come to a small house. The pastor's wife dismounts and ties the boy to a peg in the wall. She walks to the door and knocks. A man comes out and gives her a cordial reception, whereupon he leads her into the house.

When they have disappeared, the lad unties the bridle from the peg, manages to get it off and puts it in his pocket. He then creeps upon the house and through a slit in the roof observes what goes on inside. He sees twelve women sitting at a table, and the man who came out is the thirteenth. He recognizes his mistress in there. He notes that the women have great respect for this man to whom they are relating their skills in magic. Thus the pastor's wife reports that she came riding on a living man. The master of the house is greatly impressed and remarks that it is an exceptionally powerful witchcraft to ride a living man. She will be an outstanding magician, he says, "for this I never knew anyone capable of except myself." The other women are excited by this and ask him to teach them this art. He then lays out a book, grey in color and written with fire or fire-colored letters. The gleam that emanates from the letters is the only light in the house. The master now starts to teach the content of this book to the women and the boy absorbs everything he demonstrates.

As the day dawns, the women say it is time to go. At that, the teaching stops and each woman pulls out a glass and hands it to the master. The boy notes that the glasses contain something reddish which the master imbibes. He then returns the glasses to the women. After that they take leave of him with great affection and respect and exit from the house. The boy sees that each woman has her own bridle and a mount: one has a horse's leg bone, another a jaw bone, the third a shoulder bone, etc. Each takes her mount and rides away. As to the pastor's wife, she does not find her mount and is running in wild frenzy around the house when, without a warning, the lad jumps down from the roof and manages to get the bridle on her. He then mounts her and rides back home. After the night's lesson, he is able to steer the pastor's wife on the right path and nothing worth reporting happens during their journey, until they return to the stable from which they had set out. There, the lad dismounts and ties the pastor's wife on a stall. He then walks to the house and reports the night's happenings and the whereabouts of the pastor's wife. Everybody is startled by his story, not the least the pastor. The pastor's wife is now fetched and interrogated. She finally admits that for some years she and eleven other pastors' wives have attended the School of Black Arts, where Satan himself taught them magic, and that they'd had only one more year of studies left. She says that he had claimed their menstrual blood in return for his teaching and this had been the red stuff that the lad saw in the glasses. The pastor's wife is then subjected to deserved punishment for her evil.

INTERPRETATION

German goddess Frîja riding on a broom-stick

———

wall painting in the Schleswig Cathedral
photo by Toni Schneiders in *Larousse World Mythology*, p. 388

"Know Thyself"

In popular belief, the witch's vehicle is the broom. A wall painting in the Schleswig Cathedral shows the German goddess Frîja riding on a broom-stick. Frîja was the wife of Wodan. In Norse mythology, she is known as Frigg, wife of Odin. The Germanic peoples seemingly saw Frîja as their Venus, for as the Romans consecrated Friday to the goddess of love and called it *dies Veneris* so it was called *frîatag* in Old High German.[1] As to the English version, *Friday* (*fredag* in the Scandinavian languages), it remains open to question whether it is named for Frigg or Freyja. But as in Norse mythology, it is Freyja who is cast in the Venusian role as goddess of love and fertility, she seems to be the more likely candidate. In the context of our tale, it

---

1   Simek, p. 78.

is worth noting that both Frigg and Freyja owned a falcon dress and hence were able to fly. It seems pretty clear that Frigg and Freyja represented two aspects of the one original goddess. Freyja is frequently portrayed as Odin's mistress while Frigg is his wife and mother of his son, Baldur. Apparently the *völva* and the mother of the son could not be reconciled in the wife. Katla's conflict in the previous tale bears witness to this split and the consequent repression of the *völva*. We see its effect again in "The Witch's Ride" where the gifted woman should have contented herself with being a pastor's beloved wife.

The tale emphasizes the magic of menstruation and the fear of its revolutionary power, seen, of course, as evil. The stable boy unveils the menstruants in the eleventh hour. In but one year the pastors' wives would have become masters of satanic arts and a threat to the established order. The tale's thinly disguised sexual overtones evoke a power struggle that reaches back to Adam and his first wife, Lilith, who came to represent the female created at the same time as the male in Genesis 1:

> Then God said, "Let us make man in our image, according to our likeness: let them have dominion over the fish of the sea, over the birds of the air, and over the cattle, over all the earth and over every creeping thing that creeps on the earth." So God created man in his *own* image; in the image of God he created him; male and female he created them.[2]

Adam is said to have favored the missionary position in sex, but Lilith pointed out that she was his equal and refused to lie beneath him. In *Eve: A Biography*, Pamela Norris relates that "when Adam threatened to overpower Lilith by force, she uttered the magic name of God and flew away to the Red Sea [...] where she lived with a horde of lascivious demons and became renowned for her promiscuity."[3]

---

2   26-27.

3   P. 278.

We note that Lilith has an intimate knowledge of God—she utters the sacred name which according to tradition is an unpronounceable mystery and considered by Kabbalists to be a formula of creation.[4] We also note that she has the ability to fly and that the Red Sea, as a metaphor for menstrual blood, is a breeding pool for evil. For the alchemists on the other hand "the term 'our Red Sea' refers to the *aqua permanens*, the universal solvent—that is, the liquid form of the Philosopher's Stone" which was the alchemists' ultimate goal.[5] Yet again we are reminded of Philaletes' reference to the "menstruum of a whore" as the *prima materia* from which the alchemists endeavored to extract the "Royal Diadem." And it is worth repeating that *menstruum* as "solvent" refers to an "alchemical comparison between base metal being transmuted into gold and the supposed action of the menses" (see Page 7). The implication is that we must let our petrified habits and outdated worldviews dissolve in the dark chaos of the "Red Sea" in order to find our true selves. Woman is thus not to turn her back on the potential inherent in her menstrual flow but to shine light on and transform her demons into guides and helpers. "Know thyself" was written over the entrance to the oracle at Delphi. The thorny path toward that end was recognized by our distant ancestors as the ultimate goal of education.

When we enter a university, we are met with an inscription in golden letters that reads "Education is Power." "The Witch's Ride" supports this universal dictum. In spite of its humorous tone, the tale exposes the primitive fear of female wisdom and menstrual power. It also discloses that education sanctioned by the ruling powers is selective and was, at the time of "The Witch's Ride," the province of males. In fact, the same may be applied to magical knowledge, for it is seen as an asset in the case of the stable boy but is regarded as evil in the hands of the women. The latter were the severely repressed race and, as a consequence, they were feared like dynamite.

---

4   Pollack, p. 265.

5   Edinger, p. 72.

The Wolf in the Woods

The expression "riding the rag" is a dethroning of the menstruating female in the spirit of the grotesque philosophy of the middle ages. Laughter became man's response to that over which he had no power. In an introduction to our tale, a "witch's ride," in Icelandic *gandreid*, is said to have "referred originally to riding wolves, and wolves were ridden by giantesses as is related in both the elder and the younger Edda."[6] One such example is the account of Hyrrokkin who came to the gods' rescue at Baldur's funeral. Baldur "the good" was Odin's beloved son whose death foreshadowed the end of the latter's reign. When the gods could not budge Baldur's great ship on which his cremation was to take place, they sent for Hyrrokkin, who came riding on a wolf bridled with a snake and with one push sent the vessel sailing.

In *Völuspá in skamma* ("Short Prophecy of the Seeress"), the origin of *völvas* is traced to *Vidólf,* that is, to the "wolf in the woods." We should pause for a moment and consider the predicament of our bleeding foremothers in the natural habitat they shared with the wolf and other wild animals. We can imagine that these women must have had to develop survival skills that consisted in an intimate knowledge of the ways of the wolf and its acute sensitivity. In order to protect their groups from the onslaught of these animals, they would keep apart and face their fate alone. This hard-won training they were able to transfer to the exploring of perilous inner regions in the service of their community. The images of wolf-riding giantesses in sagas and myths echo a distant memory of those strong females who, like the wolf, were attuned to their instincts from which they drew strength and who rode the wild power of their menstrual blood with fearless dignity but were not swallowed by it.

But then we have Red Riding Hood who was swallowed by the wolf. The heroine of that familiar initiation tale, however, jumps

---

6   Árnason, I, p. 426.

reborn out of the wolf's belly, affirming that the growth process of feminine nature is an unbroken chain of death and rebirth. In this, as in other initiation tales, the grandmother (or her representative) attends to the girl's crossing over. She journeys with her through the dark grave of the wolf's belly and imparts to her the wisdom of bygone generations. In essence, there is nothing to fear. Death is but a transition to a more mature stage.

There is an amusing discrepancy in the Icelandic version of this tale: Little Red Riding Hood is sent with a wheat cake and a *jar of butter* to grandma, but when the pair of them are out of the wolf's belly "grandma ate the cake and drank the *wine* that Red Riding Hood had brought her."[7] Does grandma's solo celebration call to mind the red stuff imbibed by the teacher in our tale? A further discrepancy arouses the suspicion that, despite the tale's purging to befit its edifying purpose, remnants of a wolf-riding giantess still adhere to Red Riding Hood when we read that the scared "little" thing went to fetch "large and heavy stones" to put in the wolf's belly. But Red Riding Hood has learned her lesson and obediently vows never to stray off the road again and run into the woods. And why would she not make such a vow, considering the punishment dealt the pastor's wife and her wise sisters through the ages?

The wolf has an apocalyptic association in Norse mythology. The gods, who feared the wolf, tricked it into letting itself be bound. But in *Völuspá* ("Prophecy of the Seeress") the *völva* foresees that it will break loose and that Odin will meet his end in the wolf's gaping jaws as the world goes under. The bearer of bad news, the *völva* was silenced and forced underground. There is however hope in her prophecy, for she also foresaw that the earth, green and virgin, will rise out of the ocean anew.

---

7   Thorsteinsson, p. 58-62.

The Völva's Staff

Later, *gandreid* came to be used not only to denote riding on wild animals but also any journeying where magic was involved. The word is a compound of *gand* which means "mount" but also denotes the "staff," which was the attribute of the *völva*, and *reid* meaning "ride." What we have is a transition from the natural to the symbolic. The staff is an emblem of power, worldly or spiritual, as in the case of a bishop or a pope. We see it as a phallic symbol. But what does that imply in the hands of a *völva*? Considering its association with the wolf it seemingly betokens channeling of wild energy.

In his autobiography, Carl Jung relates a dream he had at the age of three or four which was to preoccupy him all his life. It was a dream in which, as he understood decades later, he had seen a "ritual phallus." In this dream, he was in a meadow and "suddenly discovered a dark, rectangular, stone-lined hole in the ground... with a stairway leading down." Fearful, he descended and came into a rectangular underground chamber, where

> in the center a red carpet ran from the entrance to a low platform. On this platform stood a wonderfully rich golden throne. I am not certain, but perhaps a red cushion lay on the seat. It was a magnificent throne, a real king's throne in a fairy tale. Something was standing on it which I thought at first was a tree trunk twelve to fifteen feet high and about one and a half to two feet thick. It was a huge thing, reaching almost to the ceiling. But it was of a curious composition: it was made of skin and naked flesh, and on top there was something like a rounded head with no face and no hair. On the very top of the head was a single eye, gazing motionlessly upward.
>
> It was fairly light in the room, although there were no windows and no apparent source of light. Above the head, however, was an aura of brightness. The thing did not move, yet I had the feeling that it might at any moment crawl off the throne like a worm and creep toward me. I was paralyzed with terror. At that moment I heard from

outside and above me my mother's voice. She called out,
"Yes, just look at him. That is the man-eater!"

Jung came to the conclusion that "at all events, the phallus of this
dream seems to be a subterranean God 'not to be named.'"[8] Could it
be that the *völva's gand*, her ritual staff, symbolized the subterranean
God in Jung's dream? "Who spoke to me then?" he asks himself.
"Who spoke to me of problems far beyond my knowledge?" And he
was only a three- or four- year-old boy. Similarly, we could ask: Who
spoke to the *völva*? How could she reveal things unknown? This
is a mystery we encounter in dreams, myths, and fairy tales. How
did our ancestors intuit hidden realities later to be confirmed by
science?

Shuttle and Redgrove suggest that in his dream Jung entered
a womb place. They argue that a phallus does not have a round
head but an urethral groove, while the cervix of the womb has a
round head. It is what inside the woman most resembles a phallus,
particularly at menstruation, when it ejaculates blood.[9] The carpet
leading to the throne, Jung emphasizes in his reflections, was *blood-
red*. He associates the thing with a worm and hears his mother's
voice say that it is "the man-eater." In the passage on "The Voice of
Truth" in Chapter 4, I elaborated on the snake as an embodiment
of the opposites of matter and spirit and referred to Judith Grahn's
observation that Western minds have been taught to see the snake
as penile, although when swallowing food, it appears vaginal. Might
we suggest that the subterranean God "not to be named" in Jung's
dream was the bisexual God who speaks in Genesis 1? The God who
created man in his *own* image, male and female? And that it was to
this bisexual phenomenon, the dual nature of woman's sexual make-
up that the *völva's* staff referred? *Heidur* is the name given to *völvas* in
the sagas. It is a masculine noun meaning "honor" and as an adjective

---

8   1989, pp. 11-13.

9   P. 102.

refers to the "cloudless" sky. As such, it hints at the *völva's* bisexual nature and bears witness to the high regard in which those women were held as a channel for the energy that spoke through them.

Jung experienced his dream as an initiation into the secrets of the earth. The myth about Freyja's descent into the stone where she acquired Brísingamen is in my mind a complementary experience to his. Jung's definition of God rhymes with the effects I suspect the *völva's* prophecies had on Odin: "This is the name by which I designate all things which cross my willful path violently and recklessly, all things which upset my subjective views, plans and intentions and change the course of my life for better or worse."[10] That, I imagine, was why Odin, the male side of the equation, felt that he had to take charge and rob the *völva* of her natural powers. A stone carving in the Swedish History Museum shows Odin riding on his eight-legged steed, Sleipnir, with a cup in his hand and spear flying over his head, reflecting his dual nature as poet and god of war.[11] It seems to me that the ironic tone of "The Witch's Ride" alludes to Odin's theft of the "mead of poetry" from Gunnlöd and the reversal of roles it entailed. Whereas Freyja was the one who taught *seiðr* to Odin, we now have a male figure in the role of the master while the woman is tied on a stall like livestock.

Eventually, the broom replaced the *völva's* staff as the witch's vehicle. While indicating a narrowing of the female sphere of action, it also connected the power invested in the *gand* to actual women's lives. In China, "riding a horse" is one metaphor for the "month-period."[12] In our tale, the pastors' wives ride the bones of a dismembered horse. In one sense this imagery implies the dissolving phase of the menstrual flow. It also refers to the horse as a sacrificial

---

10   Elder, p. 327; quoted from *Letters* 2.525.

11   The image and a short text about Sleipnir, written for ARAS (Archive for Archetypal Symbolism), is accessible on my website www.dreamsandtarot.is.

12   Eberhard, p. 186.

animal in Norse heathendom. The horse was sacred and intimately linked with the gods, particularly Odin and Freyr. The mid-winter sacrificial celebration was called yule (Ice. *jól*), a denomination that was transferred onto Christmas as the celebration of the birth of Jesus. The timing of the pastors' wives' escapade puts menstruation in a religious and spiritual context. The heathen sacrificial celebration took place on a date determined by the lunar calendar, which counted thirteen moons. The thirteenth person at the table in the School of Black Arts, the master himself, would thus refer to the moon. Looks like that "old giant" Suttungr, whom Odin deprived of his drink when he stole the mead of poetry from Gunnlöd (see Page 8off), is brought back to life in this tale. What "The Witch's Ride" appears to irreverently present to us is the underside of Jesus and his twelve disciples who, according to tradition, were all males. Which begs the question, why were they 13? And what was Judas's role within that number? Was Jesus maybe the avatar of the Sun and Judas an incarnation of the dark Moon?

Menstruation and Sacrifice

Given the allusion to the heathen sacrificial ceremony, it is interesting to explore the connection between menstruation and sacrifice. "The term sacrifice derives from the Latin *sacrificium*, which is a combination of the words *sacer*, meaning something set apart from the secular or profane for the use of supernatural powers, and *facere*, meaning 'to make.' "[13] It is tempting to apply this definition to menstrual seclusion during which woman became an instrument for the supernatural in furthering human evolution and development. Tales like "Katla's Dream" suggest that such a pattern may be engrained in the memory of the collective psyche (Chapter 5). Her sleep for four days within an invisible protective circle led to

---

13   *Encyclopaedia Britannica.*

a positive change in her culture. If indeed the Delphic oracle, which operated once a month, was associated with the sibyl's menstrual moment, this makes good sense. As stated by Shuttle and Redgrove, "no political action was ever taken even in classical Greece without consultation with the Sibylline oracle."[14] The lesson this imparts to us as individuals is to withdraw from the chatter of our programmed minds in the face of an important decision and give credence to the voice of our authentic self. We recall the exhortation "Know thyself" above the entrance to Delphi. Through self-knowledge, we withdraw the projections of our demons onto others, and the world becomes a more peaceful place.

Descriptions of sacrificial rituals in the sagas bear a striking likeness to women's bloodshed and point to the womb as the original sacrificial vessel. The sacrificial place was called *hof*, which originally meant "mound" (cf. Venusian mound). The blood of the animal was poured into a cup which stood on a stone altar in the innermost part of the sanctuary. On the altar was also a ring at which oaths were sworn. (I refer to Freyja's Brísinga*men* and to the necklace [*men*] that Kári gave to Katla, also referred to as a ring). Standing in the cup was a rod with which the blood was smeared on the altar and on the inside and outside walls of the *hof.* Then it was sprinkled on the participants. The meat was cooked and ale was in ample supply. The gods were toasted: Odin, Njord, Freyr... no mention is made of goddesses.[15] The belief that sacrifice releases energy and brings about increased fruitfulness could be deduced from woman's biological function. It seems logical that man's sacrificial celebration in mid-winter should be inspired by the ritual established by Freyja and honored by her human daughters who withdrew from the world like the fading sunlight in winter, pulled into the sacred temple of their bodies, and returned cleansed, invigorated and fertile like the virgin soil in spring.

---

14   P, 147.

15   "Hákonar saga góða," ch. 14, in Snorri Sturluson's *Heimskringla*, I ; *Eyrbyggja saga*, ch. 4.

Horse as Symbol

The horse is invested with power that man has been able to harness and make work for him. Symbolically, rider and horse denote ego and instinct where, ideally, the former holds the reins and is in command. Our tale betrays an anxious concern that the ego part be played by the male. "The data of prehistoric archeology shows that the ancient tribes of our part of the world believed that a principle of the divine nature existed in the horse."[16] This is certainly true of Sleipnir, who bore the god between the upper and the nether worlds. By eating the meat of the sacrificed animal, man partook of its divine nature. When Icelanders adopted Christianity, they were permitted to practice, in secret, the heathen custom of eating horse meat. Later, during centuries of hardship and hunger, annals reveal that the population preferred death from starvation rather than resort to eating horse meat. It appears that the wine and the bread as symbol for the blood and body of the sacrificed Redeemer had taken root in the psyche and prohibited regression to more primitive customs.

Blood as Sacrament

But what of the cake and the wine eaten by Red Riding Hood's grandma after their joint journey through the dark grave of the wolf's belly? This is a symbolic sacrament which is made literal in The Witch's Ride. Thereby woman's regression during her period is emphasized in a negative manner. The spiritual powers with whom she consorted within the sacred boundaries of her ritual seclusion, have taken on the identity of Satan. It is no doubt meaningful that the pastor's wife in our tale is not a mother. What is sacrificed in menstruation, according to primitive belief, is the potential child. By juxtaposing the blood offered by the women to Satan and the birth

---

16   Charbonneau-Lassay, p. 96.

of Jesus, the tale intimates that Christ's voluntary sacrifice cleansed the human race of the stain of menstrual blood which ushered us into consciousness as a species. On a mundane level, Christ's role could be compared to that of the midwife who brought us into the light and cleansed us of our mothers' lochial blood. Between that moment and the hour of death lies the path laid out by Jesus. The problem is that on that path menstruation does not come into play, that is to say, not in a natural way. The bleeding vulva is hinted at in the wound in the side of the male Christ through which he gave birth to the church while woman's menstruation was relegated to the shadows as our tale shows all too clearly.

The death inherent in the menstrual blood is overridden by the birth of the Son who bestowed eternal life on mankind. By surrendering himself to God's will that he be sacrificed in order to redeem the human race, Christ taught by example and conquered death. It is the fear of death that keeps us from living our full potential. We are afraid to stray away from the path laid out for us lest we should be torn apart by the wolf in the woods. This fear is a potent weapon in the hands of rulers. Christ was a revolutionary sentenced to death by the ruling powers of his time. So was Joan of Arc and countless other wise women in the dark Middle Ages. The punishment dealt the pastor's wife in our tale is left to our imagination.

The idea that "through sacrifice, life is returned to its divine source, regenerating the power or life of that source," takes on a sinister meaning in our tale. [17] What is alluded to is that by tuning into the power and wisdom of her nature, woman sustains the life of the Devil and increases his power. "The Witch's Ride" is thus another version of the vampire story, with one important difference though: the women in this tale are agents, not victims in need of being saved from themselves by a hero. Like Eve, they are driven by desire for knowledge.

---

17   *Encyclopaedia Britannica.*

7
The Farmer at Fossvellir

from *Icelandic Folk and Fairy Tales*, III
collected by Jón Árnason

The storyteller's switching between the past and present
tense has for the most part been left intact.

Foss means "waterfall" in Icelandic. The name of the farm
is derived from its location on fields by a waterfall. The
events are believed to have taken place in the eighteenth
century.

In earlier times, a farmer lived at Fossvellir on *Langanes* ("long-
point"). The farm was located a short distance from *Saudanes*
("wether-point"), but is now deserted. This farmer had many
young children of whom the eldest was a daughter. It was her task at

night to drive the milch ewes out to the Foss-river, which cascades down from the heath, not far from the farm. In late summer, the girl complained to her father that she had been pursued by a rock giant for two nights in a row. Crying, she begged him not to make her drive the ewes the third night. The father became angry and accused her of making this up in order to get out of tending the ewes. "You will, nonetheless, drive the ewes tonight," he said. So that is how it had to be and she took the ewes out to the Foss-river that evening.

When the girl is not back at bedtime, the farmer begins to suspect that his daughter has been telling the truth. He sets out to the Foss-river, but the girl is nowhere to be seen. He returns devastated by sorrow and regret. At dawn the following day, he rides over to Saudanes, to see the pastor who resided there, and gives him a detailed account of the situation. The pastor says that he cannot free her from the giants to whom she has been bewitched—"and we must, without delay," says he, "send a messenger up north to *Múli* ('projecting mountain'), to the pastor there who is my brother. He will be able to have your daughter released." At that, the pastor writes a letter and expedites it with a messenger to his brother. The messenger arrives at Múli and delivers the letter, along with the Saudanes-pastor's greeting. The pastor reads the letter and says: "These are bad news, for the farmer's daughter is in the hands of the most evil giants[1] here in the north. If we have not arrived before three suns have set at Saudanes, these evil beings will have bewitched her so potently that it will be beyond repair." Having said this, the pastor prepares in haste to leave with the messenger.

They ride night and day and manage every time to exchange their worn-out horses for fresh ones. Even so, they did not arrive at Saudanes until three days had passed. Then the Múli-minister

---

1   The term used as a collective for the giants in the tale is the neuter *tröll* which refers to both male and female.

said it was already too late. They nonetheless gave in to the farmer's pleading, and both clergymen went with him to the Foss-river and to the waterfall that is in the river. The Múli-minister pulls out a wand and strikes on the rock. At that, a large door opens into a cave. The pastor conjures the one who is in charge to appear and, immediately, a dreadful giant comes to the door. The pastor asks if he has abducted the farmer's daughter. The giant says that this is true. "Let us see her!" the clergyman says. The giants then let her come to the door with an iron chain around her waist.

The clergymen are taken aback by her fearful looks. She has become big like a giant and blue like Hel[2]. No human resemblance was to be seen except the baptismal-cross on her forehead which was white and with natural skin color. When she sees her father, she asks the giants to allow her to kill him, for he is to blame for all her misfortune. But the Múli-minister orders her to go back into the cave and never again come before the eyes of man.

The Múli-minister then asked the rock-giant: "Are there many giants in your cave and what do they live on?" The giant replied: "We are five and get our food from a lake full of fish in our cave." The pastor then conjures the giant to go back in. The cave closed on his heels and the minister stepped away from the door.

It is rumored among wise men that red runestaves are still to be seen on the rock, in the place where the door was. But as he witnessed this whole event, the farmer became overwhelmed by sorrow and lived but a short time afterwards. Following this, farming was discontinued at Fossvellir, and nobody has lived there ever since.

---

2   The goddess of death in Norse mythology who was half blue and half skin color.

Broddadals-river.
On its banks stands the farm
where my grandmother
was born.

INTERPRETATION

The Daughter Within Me

I have come to understand why the fate of the farmer's daughter in this tale has had such a hold on me. Behind my drive to free her is the need to liberate a daughter in myself whom I locked away in my innermost temple. I intended it as punishment for her, but it turned against myself and banned my access to the sacred source.

> *I am a young girl*
> *tumbling on a chair in*
> *the kitchen nook*
> *oblivious*
> *of my*
> *torn*
> *panties*
> *when his anger, his*
> *indignation*
> *hit me*
> *like*

an unstoppable
force.
Indecent girl!
Bewildered
my laughter quenched
I curl up in shame
defenseless
frozen
she sinks
underground
my young vulva, my
enemy
I became two.
Oh, I hated that girl.
The rejection turned against
myself
with vehemence, with
rage
I screamed every time
she stirred up the
memory,
why did you do it!
go away, get lost, go to the
bottom of the
sea!

My mission to free the daughter of the farmer at Fossvellir is an act of redemption for the cruelty I vented on the girl in myself who stood on the threshold of puberty. The fate of the farmer's daughter makes me understand that my painful experience is rooted in the collective, driving both him who caused the wound and me, the wounded, who perpetuated it. It forces me to look my alliance with the repressive powers in the eye. Not without pain do I see in the Múli-minister's banishment the reflection of my own attitude toward the girl I expelled to the bottom of the sea for having accidentally exposed herself in the kitchen nook of my childhood. She became one with my vulva—with my awakening sexuality—that thoughtless girl. Became one with that moment of disgust and rejection. Later, much later, I understood that the curse she brought on herself might have been the projection of illegitimate stirrings in the other. But I only saw her consuming guilt. She was the culprit. The reactions she triggered made that clear to me.

Where is the Mother?

The question the tale endeavors to answer is: Why did Fossvellir fall into desolation? It strikes me right away that there is no mention of a mother, whether deceased or alive. Then it occurs to me that the mother element may be projected on the milch ewes and the heath from which the Foss-river cascades. *Heath* is *heidi* in Icelandic, and like the English word it is related to "heathen=heath dwellers." It also evokes the name *Heidur*, which was given to the *völvas*, the prophetesses, in the old sagas. This is the home of rock giants, powerful forces reviled as evil by the Múli-minister. On the one hand are the nourishing milch ewes and on the other, raw uncouth power, the very opposites man projected on woman as mother and menstruant. It seems to me that the farmer's daughter is terrified of the impersonal power that resides in her but she experiences as coming from outside. She wants to run away from it, but it is bound to catch up with her as it caught up with Thorn-Rose in spite of her father's precautions. Can we help but notice how different this tale is from Freyja's initiation in the stone on which it is no doubt founded?

The daughter blames her father for her misfortune. How would it have changed the outcome if the father had listened to his daughter's intuition? Did the daughter foresee the dire consequences her father's denial would have? That it would lead to ruin? Do we detect in this tale an echo of *Völuspá* ("Prophecy of the Seeress"), a poem that has lived with the Icelandic people since before the conversion to Christendom? In this timeless poem, the *völva* foresees a world torn by corruption and war where brothers will kill each other and family ties be severed, where no one will spare another before the world goes under.[3] "The Farmer at Fossvellir" is testimony to the denial of the ruling powers in the face of the *völva's* age-old warnings. The tale reveals an irreconcilable split between the earthly and heavenly powers that, once upon a time, were one and should, ideally, be in a harmonious relationship with one another. Maybe the farm's falling into desolation is a microcosmic reflection of the apocalyptic end of a corrupt world prophesied by the *völva*. At the end of the poem, she announces that she will go under, as if she foresaw that her voice would be stilled. The Múli-minister may seem to fulfill her prophecy by silencing the farmer's daughter. Could maybe, in fact, this be the genesis of her anger—i.e. from the denial of a prophetic gift which we have come to see associated with menstruation in previous tales?

Cultural and Mythological Background

The tale reveals an acute tension between the heathen past and the Lutheran church some eight hundred years after Christianization. The farmer and his daughter are but powerless pawns between these contending parties. As I have described in my interpretation of "The 'Hidden Woman' in Hafnanúpur," the 18th century, when the events described in the tale were believed to have taken place, was a dismal period in the history of the Icelandic people. The previous century, sometimes referred to as the age of witchcraft, had been marked by burnings at the stake. In the pulpits, nature in its broadest sense was reviled as the devil's playfield and the vigilant eye of a punishing god upheld as a deterrent against the sins of the flesh. I have described in Chapter 1, that at some point in time, woman became ensnared between the worldview of our agricultural ancestors who were attuned to the cyclicity inherent in nature, and the heroic worldview enforced by Odin. Our tale reveals that she

---

3   St. 44.

is now caught between her inherent nature and the servants of a Christian god. But here we have a totally different outlook toward feminine power which was, after all, valued in Odin's world despite the fact that he sought to take control of it and appropriate it to his own ends. Because its value was recognized, the Æsir were fearful of losing Freyja to the giants. *Idun* ("she who renews"), wife of Bragi the god of poetry, was another goddess whom they feared losing to those desirous mountain dwellers, for she guarded apples in her ashen box that kept them forever young. But the ministers do not care at all about the menstruous farmer's daughter; they just want to silence her once and for all. The gate between heaven and hell is slammed shut with the damned trapped in matter. The aspect of the feminine, personified by the daughter, is deemed beyond redemption by the Múli-minister. I have made it my task to prove him wrong.

The tale presents the father figure on two levels: the earthy farmer on the one hand and the spiritual fathers, representatives of the heavenly father, on the other. The latter claim that the daughter is a victim of enchantment by evil forces. This is emphasized through repetition and hints at woman's legendary lack of steadfastness in the face of evil. Her accusations against her father are silenced by the reverend father. Not only is she a threat, I suspect, to her own father but also to the church fathers and to the general image of the Father with all the power invested in it.

Underlying this tale, staged on the human plane on a specific Icelandic farm, is an archetypal pattern. Just as the mother of Freyja is hidden from view in the myths, so too is the mother of the farmer's daughter in the tale. Freyja's father, the fertility god Njord, was the archetypal farmer. Again, the fertility cult was based on the cyclic rhythm of the moon and the seasons, the cycle of death and rebirth, which is echoed in the menstrual cycle and cast in gold in Freyja's Brísingamen as a symbol for this feminine reality. As you will recall, Freyja acquired her jewel, as recorded by Catholic priests, by sleeping for four consecutive nights with four dwarfs who had their abode in a rock. It does not take much ingenuity to see the common motif behind the folk tale "The Farmer at Fossvellir" and the myth about Freyja's affair with the dwarfs. Dwarf or giant, both were associated with the moon and menstruation (see Page 27).

There exists in ancient poetry a reference to *Máni* ("moon") as a giant, which appears to be derived from a lost myth. A lost myth raises suspicion. It seems clear that the moon was experienced as the primary source of divine energy before the aggressive Æsir, incarnations of the solar principle, won out over the fertility deities of peace and plenty. This was probably why Máni, as the consort of Freyja and her human daughters, had to be exiled and dropped from myth. One scholar remarks that Máni's fate at *Ragnarök*, "the end of the world created by Odin," is not explicitly stated. As part of that creation, he speculates, Máni must have been destroyed like the rest.[4] This has me thinking. In the next to the last stanza of the *Prophecy*, the *völva* announces that a powerful being, an absolute ruler, will come from above to pronounce judgement.[5] This, I imagine, will be the moment when gods and men have to look themselves in the eye. Curiously, scholars have tended to exclude this verse because they cannot make it fit in. This again raises suspicion. I tend to think that this powerful ruler is a reference to the moon and its everlasting cyclicity to which the female is intimately bound. The moon being the mirror of the sun, it reflects back to the conscious being the deep and buried stuff that it has to reckon with before it can ascend to the next plane. A new cycle is announced by the *völva* who sees the green earth arise again out of the apocalyptic chaos. A new era will be ushered in where division and enmity will be replaced by unity restored. Her prophecy is an appeal to a misguided humanity, a message that has seemingly escaped the Múli-minister

4   Lindow, p. 223.

5   St. 65 in Nordal.

as is betrayed by his contemptuous attitude towards the spirit that inhabits the material world. He is a representative of an almighty god in the heaven up above who, under the auspices of the ecclesiastical establishment, had become divorced from nature. The monstrosity of the farmer's daughter in the eyes of the clergymen in the folk tale bespeaks patriarchy's attitude towards woman's menstrual nature, held sacred by the fertility cults of old. Her gift, symbolized before by a gold necklace, has become a curse, betokened by an iron chain by which she is bound to primitive, mortal nature. In his endeavor to oust menstrual power for good and all, the Múli-minister joins forces with the fairy tale king, Thorn-Rose's father, and the modern day proponents of menstrual suppression. The consequences are reflected in the desolate end of the story.

Lake Full of Fish

What are we to make of the lake full of fish that feeds the giants in the cave? I would not be surprised at all if it were of the same substance as the mead of poetry that Odin stole from Gunnlöd, that is, the living source at the root of being (see Chapter 4). The fish is a symbol of fertility and the origin of life. Before it became sacramental food in the Christian tradition, it was associated with the great goddesses of the fertility cults. Many a folk tale relates how the dream of a sterile queen leads her towards a stream where she is to catch and eat a fish that will restore her fertility. The folk tale points the way for me. I have become convinced that liberating the daughter is my key to the living water.

Pursuing my train of thought, I pull the Page of Cups from a Tarot deck. What do I see? The *cup of inspiration* in the hands of a young boy (see image). Gradually, it begins to feel like an auspicious synchronicity in the context of the subject I am dealing with. In my experience, tarot cards tend to provide keys that can unlock mysteries that I am grappling with. The dialogue that ensues

PAGE OF CUPS

between the card and female initiation opens up a new meaning that I had not hitherto seen. The card on which my drawing is based comes from the Rider-Waite-Smith deck that was published in 1909 and the design of which is inevitably influenced by the zeitgeist of its time. It is still by far the most widely used deck worldwide, but, in more recent decks, the Pages have often been traded out for a female character, such as a Princess, in an effort to balance the masculine bias people have seen in the court cards where the Queen is the only female presentation in a family of four, encompassing, besides her, a Page, a Knight and a King.

The Pages are young and hint at something new being seeded in the mind and life of the querent. Those who are familiar with the cards will know that the Page energy can make itself felt in us at one time or another, regardless of gender, and regardless of age. The Page of Cups is latent or alive in us all. But what of a young girl who encounters the *cup of inspiration* in the hands of a boy? Might she not think that the gift the card holds out is meant for her brother rather than for herself? Might it not impart to her the message that creative inspiration is the province of males? Pages are students, and the seeds sown in the Page cards need to be cultivated with passion in order to bring their promise to fruition. If a girl comes face-to-face with the Page of Cups and feels an attraction, she will need to be able to own the energy. If she cannot do that, she might project envy onto her brother who seemingly has it in his hands, or become the lover-muse of an aspiring poet or artist, rather than pursue her own creative path. As the concept of a muse is traditionally projected on the female, it might not come to her so readily to see the boy in the card as her muse. However, by virtue of his name, which means "poetry, poem," this was the role *Od* must have played for Freyja.

The youth's focus is on the fish popping out of the golden cup. If I were reading this card for a girl being initiated into adulthood,

I would see an awakening to the voice of spirit within as separate from her own voice conditioned by her education and upbringing. As the fish pops up from the deep waters of her unconscious, so the lotus flowers adorning her tunic rise out of muddy soil, evoking her menstrual blood as a fertilizer for her flowering as a woman. Her agricultural foremothers, I would tell her, used their blood for precisely those purposes with stunning results, as fertilizer for their crops. Besides, it was held to have curative properties, and was used as a love potion to boot. Cup-shaped on a long phallic stem, those lotus flowers echo the blue fish as a phallic symbol in the golden cup and hint at the androgyny inherent in nature, within as without. So, too, do the red and blue colors of her dress. She does not need to confine herself to the traditional roles her culture has cut out for a woman. Now that her future lies wide open before her, I would point out the attention with which the youth listens to the spirit messenger come from the depths. It is from those depths that her personal truth and talents unfold. The indication of a "third eye" on the Page's hat points to visionary talent and creative imagination. These are gifts nature bestows on menarcheal girls, which should be nurtured but of which, as the folktale "The Farmer at Fossvellir" brings into the open, they were consistently robbed through demonization of their menstrual nature.

The Cave and the High Priestess

The folk tale takes me beyond the established sanctuary of a church to the cave, held sacred by the ancestors as the symbolic womb from which our species emerged at the dawn of civilization. As the place of our common origin, the cave imparts a feeling of unity and equality. The attitude of the clergymen, on the other hand, is dialectic and exclusive. They oust as evil the feminine power invested in the daughter by shutting her up in the cave which, on a psychological level, lies beyond the limits of the rational mind.

In the divinatory system of tarot, the High Priestess is the source of living water. Clad in blue, with a crucifix at the heart level and crowned with the moon, she sits on a cube, either in the mouth of a cave,[6] or as on the image referred to in "The 'Hidden Woman' in Hafnanúpur," between two stone columns, with behind her the veiled mystery, which I suggested evokes the vessel guarded by Gunnlöd in Hnitbjörg (see Chapter 4). The image of the farmer's daughter in the door of the cave as seen through the eyes of the clergymen— huge, blue, awesome and in chains—looks to me like a distortion of the High Priestess on a tarot card. I am struck by the fact that the former has a baptismal cross on the forehead, which to me evokes the thinking function, while the latter bears an even-handed cross at the heart level, implying that when we find ourselves at cross roads the feeling heart should be the guide. The central point of the cross signifies the meeting of the mundane (the horizontal line) and the timeless (the vertical line), a moment of a transforming insight that is comprehended by the whole personality, not just the rational mind.

It does not seem farfetched to surmise that what is at stake for the church fathers is regression to a belief system in which a priestess, *völva* or sibyl, played the key role. As previously mentioned, *völva* (derived from Latin *vulva, volva*) and *Delphi*, where the oracle resided, mean "womb."[7] The cave, too, is an image of the womb of the earth. Through her biological make-up, woman as *völva* is the guardian of the secret of creation.

The motif behind the folktale intimates a parallel between the farmer's daughter and Freyja, who was the daughter of a fertility god and a goddess of Love. As such, Freyja stood for qualities that the flock must have seen painfully lacking in the god represented by the servants of the church. The farmer's daughter is a human incarnation of the goddess who, as I keep repeating, was publicly reviled as a *bitch*

---

6   *The Gill Tarot Deck*; the image can be seen at http://www.lepalaisdutarot.com/Tarot/Gill_Tarot_deck.jpg

7   Bolen 1994, p. 117.

by the lawmaker and Christian missionary Hjalti Skeggjason in 999 CE. The Múli-minister takes the missionary's curse a step further by locking the farmer's daughter up in the cave. According to rumor, the storyteller reports, the clergyman did so by applying rune magic, the very means for which the church persecuted the oppressed populace by fire. This gives the tale an ironic twist. The hypocrisy of the church fathers is unmasked. The parish name *Saudanes* ("wether-point") may well be another venomous dart aimed at the servants of the church. *Saudur* ("wether") is a "castrated male sheep," which by way of association would intimate the sterility of the religion the clergymen uphold, while the daughter's relationship with the milch ewes points to the abundance in nature that nourishes man.

F-Rune and Red-gold

The first rune in the runic alphabet, the f-rune, is called *fé* which in Icelandic can refer to either livestock, in particular to sheep, or monetary wealth. To the ancestors, the runic alphabet represented the order of the universe. A rune was not simply a letter, it was also a key to the mystery of creation. On an inner or spiritual level, the *fé*-rune stands for evolutionary power, the fire that drives our growth and development. The key word for this rune in an old Icelandic rune poem is *aurum*, which is Latin for "gold," and more specifically *red*-gold. We recall that the poets of old associated Freyja's tears with red-gold, an image that I have come to see as a euphemism for the menstrual blood dripping from the "weeping womb." True to the pattern, the farmer's daughter *cries* when she pleads with her father to spare her the woe that she sees approaching. This is a far cry from Freyja's attraction to Brísingamen which patriarchal culture has wrought into an iron chain. There is reason to believe that the incipient movement inherent in the *fé*-rune was brought about by the menstruation of the human female, aptly referred to by the Chinese as *the first tide*.[8]

---

8   Eberhard, p. 186.

The *red-gold* is the fire that drives a woman along a cyclic spiritual path where she has the possibility to refine her talents, to make of herself a *poem* in co-creation with her instinctual nature. That patriarchy has made every effort to bar woman from this creative source, is depicted in the folk tale "The Farmer at Fossvellir." A better known example is the biblical tale of Eve's temptation in the Garden of Eden, where the woman's initial impulse towards knowledge is attributed to machinations of the devil in the guise of a serpent who, as said before, through its rejuvenating shedding of the skin, is mythologically associated with the womb and the moon. She shall be a *victim* of her feminine nature through suffering as per God's decree addressed to the serpent: "I will put enmity between you and the woman."[9] As the serpent has come to represent the devil in the Biblical context so do the giants represent evil in this tale. The Word has tremendous power, be it in Eden or in eighteenth century Icelandic countryside.

That the masculine, which to a large extent rules our minds, needs to be in touch with its animating feminine side is borne out by our story. When the church father locked the instinctual powers up in the cave, he cut the farmer's lifeline to the wellspring at the root of his being. As a result he lost his lust for life and suffered an untimely death. The moral of the story is, that the repressive diabolization of nature upheld by the servants of the church leads to ruin. Man must own his primitive nature and deal with it consciously.

How Do I Free the Daughter?

The tale is about the farmer as is emphasized by its title. What I am concerned about is the daughter's fate. How do I free her? What rune will undo the Múli-minister's spell? I opt for the s-rune, which

---

9   Gen. 3:15.

encompasses the power of the sun. I read the sun-rune as the source of life and guiding light of consciousness. I believe that the secret inherent in this rune will melt away the ice of inertia in which the farmer's daughter is trapped. It will restore the ousted Daughter to her former status as avatar of the sun, equal to the Son, her twin and masculine counterpart. She will shine once more at the heart of being and promote love and peace amongst men and women. I will look to the Tarot Queen of Wands (see image) as a beacon on my mission to free the captive.

In the system of Tarot, Queens represent the element of water and Wands, also referred to as Staffs, the element of fire. What Freyja as *völva* represents on an archetypal level, the Queen of Wands incarnates on the human scale. Look at her, seated on an elevated throne born up by two sculpted lions. Below her you see golden mountain tops illuminated by the sun, and behind her a cloudless blue sky. She calls to mind Snorri Sturluson's description of Freyja: "When she journeys, she sits in a chariot pulled by two cats."[10] The Queen of Wands is crowned with gold and dressed in the yellow of the sun, with a tall sprouting staff in one hand and a sunflower in the other. The most important quality I see in this Queen *now* is her uninhibited awareness of her sexual power. Not only is she conscious of it, it is clear that she also feels totally at home in it. The firm grip she has on her staff shows that she knows how to channel and direct this energy in an enlightened manner. A girl at the age of puberty is unconscious of the power that resides in her, she does not know the value it has for her personal growth. As long as her feminine power is not upheld to her as a gift that she should appropriate and assimilate, she may allow herself to be robbed and exploited in myriad ways.

As I elaborated on in "The Witch's Ride," the staff was the attribute of the *völva*. And so the Wand, representing the element of

---

10   "Gylfaginning," ch. 24.

QUEEN OF WANDS

fire, distinguishes this Queen from the other Queens in the Tarot deck. She stands for one aspect of the feminine, as does the *völva*. Flaming red lions adorn the back of her throne representing wild fiery nature, while golden yellow reigns in the foreground indicating that she has transformed this primitive animal drive into light. She does not shy away from her strong emotions nor does she let herself be overpowered by them. She recognizes them as a power source that begs to be channeled into a creative act or expression. Her distant look tells me that this Queen is a visionary, she understands how the past informs the future. A black cat at her feet, alert and facing front, is the mystery in this card, her shadowy guide whom she dares trust and who steers her away from preconceptions toward the essence that lies hidden in the dark.

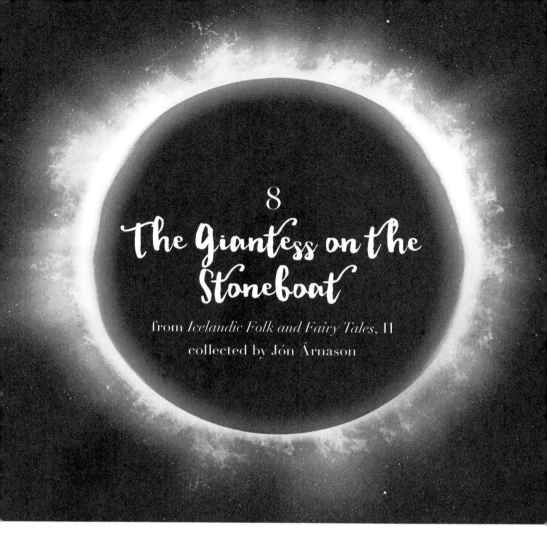

8
The Giantess on the Stoneboat

from *Icelandic Folk and Fairy Tales*, II
collected by Jón Árnason

The storyteller's switching between past and present tense
to emphasize tension and wonder has been left intact.

Once upon a time there were a king and a queen who had a son
named Sigurd. He grew up to become a peerless youth, strong,
skilled in athletics, and fine-looking. When age began to slow
the king down, he had a talk with his son and said that time had
come for him to find a good wife, for there was no knowing how
much longer he himself had to live. The son's nobility would attain
full flower, the father said, if he got a wife worthy of him. Sigurd

did not disagree and asked his father where he had in mind for him to look for a wife. The king said that in a foreign country, which he specified, there was a king who had a beautiful and promising daughter. If her father accepted Sigurd's proposal, he felt that this would be his best match.

Father and son then took leave of each other, and the prince prepared his departure. He sailed to the land his father had told him about, presented himself to the king, and asked for his daughter's hand in marriage. The king readily agreed, but on the condition that Sigurd stay there as long as he could, for the king was unwell and barely capable of ruling his kingdom. Sigurd accepted, but with the reservation that he be given permission to leave for his country when he received word that his father, who he said was old and decrepit, had passed away. Sigurd then *drank his wedding*[1] to the princess and engaged in ruling the state with his father-in-law. Sigurd and his wife loved each other dearly, and even more loving did their relationship become when a year later she gave birth to his fair and fine-looking son. Time passed. When the boy was in his second year, Sigurd received word that his father was deceased. He then prepared his departure along with his wife and son and sailed back home on one ship.

After a few days at sea and with but one day of sailing to go, they lost wind and were caught in dead calm. The ship then lay and rocked gently on the tranquil sea. The royal couple were by themselves on the deck, as everybody else had gone down below to sleep. They sat there and conversed for a while and had their son with them. After a while Sigurd became assailed by such drowsiness that he could not keep himself awake, so he went below and lay down. The queen was left all by herself up above where she played with their son.

When a good while had passed since king Sigurd had gone below, the queen sees a black spot on the sea. She notices that it

---

1   See note to the tale of Thorn-Rose explaining this archaic expression.

moves in her direction. As it comes closer to the ship she is able to figure out that this is a boat and that it is propelled by oars. She also detects some sort of a human shape in the boat. Eventually the boat pulls up to the ship and the queen sees that it is a stone boat. Next an awful and wicked-looking giantess comes aboard the ship. The queen is terrified beyond words and can neither speak nor move to awaken the king or the crew. The giantess walks towards the queen, lifts the boy from her arms and puts him down on the deck. She then strips the queen of her royal garb and leaves her standing in her underwear. The giantess now puts on the queen's clothes and by so doing, takes on human shape. Finally she puts the queen in the boat and utters this spell: "Your swift sailing shall not be halted till you arrive at my brother's in the underworld." At that, the queen sat as if paralyzed while the boat under her glided instantly away and, before long, was out of sight from the ship.

When the boat was no longer to be seen, the little prince started to cry. The giantess did not apply herself to consoling him, and even if she had, it would have been to no avail. She went with the boy on her arm down below where the king was asleep and awakens him with harsh accusations for not caring about her well-being, left alone as she has been with their son up on the deck, while he sleeps and snores and the entire crew with him. She thinks it most inconsiderate and reckless of him not to have someone stay awake with her on the ship, for there is no knowing what could happen to a person alone. Now she cannot console the boy by any means and would like to take him to where he is supposed to be, which should be possible if someone showed any drive or deed, for fair wind was blowing.

King Sigurd is taken aback by the impetuosity of his queen, who had never before spoken a cross word to him. Nonetheless he reacts kindly to her address and sympathizes with her resentment. He tries to help her console the boy, but it is to no avail. He then awakens the crew and orders sails to be hoisted, for fair wind was blowing straight to harbor. They now sailed at full speed and landed in the kingdom that Sigurd was to rule. He went to his court where everybody was in grief because of his father's passing, but now they rejoiced at having reclaimed him sound and safe. He was nominated king and became ruler of the land. The young prince hardly ever stopped crying in his mother's presence since he was left alone with her on the deck, though he had been a most tranquil child before. The king therefore had to get a nanny for him from amongst the ladies-in-waiting at the court. When the child came into the nanny's care, he quickly regained his former calm and peace.

After the voyage, the king felt that the queen had changed in many ways and not for the better. In particular, did he feel that she had become more imposing, testier, and less affable than he had expected. Yet she seemed gracious and polite, but soon it came to light that more people than the king sensed her coldness.

There were two boys at the court, one of them eighteen, the other nineteen. They had a liking for chess and spent long hours inside playing. Their chamber was adjacent to that of the queen and frequently, at certain hours of the day, they could hear her. One day they paid more attention than before to what she was saying. They put their ear to a slit in the wall between the rooms and heard clearly that the queen said: "When I yawn a small yawn, I am a little and dainty maiden, when I yawn half a yawn, I am like a half-giantess, when I yawn a whole yawn, I am like a full-fledged giantess." No sooner had she uttered these words than she was gripped by such nausea that she yawned tremendously. At this she became so startled that she immediately turned into a wicked-looking giantess. A three-headed *thurs* (giant) with a bin full of meat now came up through the floor in the queen's chamber. He greets his sister and puts the bin in front of her. She sits down and eats without halt until she has gobbled up the very last morsel. The boys witnessed everything that went on but did not hear any exchange of words between the brother and sister. They were astounded by how greedily the queen devoured the meat and how much of it she could contain and, at the same time, it no longer surprised them how little she ate when she dined with the king. When she had finished the contents of the bin, the giant disappeared down with it the same way he had come and the queen resumed human shape.

By this time, the young prince had been with the nanny for a while. One evening when she had lit a light and held the prince in her lap, it so happened that in her chamber a few floor boards broke open and a beautiful woman in her underwear came up into the room. She had an iron-ring around her waist and attached to it was a chain that reached down as far as could be seen. The woman walked over to the nanny and took the child from her, hugged him, and handed him over to the nanny again. She then went down the same way she had come and the floor closed over her head. Although the woman did not utter a word the nanny became frightened, yet she kept her calm. The next day everything went as the day before, the white-clad woman came around the same time as the previous day, took the child, caressed him and then gave him back to his nanny. But as she was about to leave she said with a sorrowful mien: "Two are gone and only one remains." Then she went down the same way again and the floor closed. Now the nanny became even more frightened than before having heard the woman speak those words. She feared that the child might be in some sort of danger, although the unknown woman had seemed kindly and had caressed the child as if he had been severed from her. What haunted the nanny in particular were the words, "and only one remains," for she thought it might mean that now there remained one of three days, as she had come to visit her for two days. The nanny resolved to go to the king and told him the whole story and asked him, by all means, to be present in her room the next day, around the time the woman was wont to come. The king promised that he would.

The following day the king came to the nanny's chamber a little before the appointed time and sat himself on a chair with a drawn sword in hand. The floor boards now broke open as before and the white-clad woman came up with the iron-ring and the chain. The king immediately recognizes his wife and without further ado cuts through the chain that trailed down from the iron-ring. This brought on such thundering bumps underground that the palace shook and trembled and nobody doubted that every house in the city would crash and crumble. When the commotion finally stopped, the king and the queen fell into each other's arms. She then told him the whole story.

She told him how the giantess had come to the ship when everybody was asleep and stripped her of her queenly garb, what she had said, and the spell she cast. She told him that when the boat, which glided on its own under her, had transported her so far away from the ship that she was no longer able to see it, she had felt as if she went through a certain blackness till the boat landed by a three-headed *thurs* who had taken her and right away wanted to sleep with her. She had flatly refused. The *thurs* then put her in an isolated house and threatened that she would never get out unless she promised him her affection. He had then paid her a visit from time-to-time. Eventually she had started to puzzle over how she might free herself from the hands of giants. She agreed to sleep with him if she were allowed to see her son above ground for three days in a row. He had consented, but girdled her with this iron-ring to which was attached this chain, one end of which he had tied around his waist. The thunderous bumps would have been caused when the king cut the chain and the giant plumped down to the bottom of the tunnel at the sudden slackening of the chain. The tremor had been so intense when he plummeted down because his home was right beneath the town. Most likely he had been killed and his death-convulsions caused the city to tremble. The queen said that she had reserved the right to see her son three days in a row because she felt it would grace her with succor and release, as had now become manifest.

The king now understood why the woman with whom he had lived for some time had been so ungracious. He immediately had a hood pulled over her head and had her beaten to death with stones. Then he had her tied to unbroken colts who tore her to pieces. With her out of the way, the youths, who had witnessed what went on in the queen's chamber, came forth and told their story. They had not dared to do so before because of her tyranny. The queen now assumes her noble role and is well-liked by all. As to the nanny, the king and the queen married her to a high ranking nobleman and provided her with a generous dowry.

INTERPRETATION

The Wonder of the Child

As a child, I puzzled over this mesmerizing tale. To me, the biggest mystery was how a stone boat could float on the sea. The fact that the street I lived on derived its name from just such a vessel somehow brought the story very close to home. And then there was the problem of the queen's double. How was it possible that the king did not realize that the giantess was not his queen? Of course I never saw them as one. The good queen was the victim of the evil giantess who merited her savage end.

Throughout my adult life, also, this tale has popped into my mind time and again. I came to feel growing empathy for the "false queen." Although I was no friend of hers as a child, as an adult I am touched by the awkwardness and unease with which she functions in her daily life at the court. As I try to put myself in her shoes, it dawns on me that she married into a culture very different from her own. I am taken aback by this realization that reveals to me how identified I am with the male-oriented worldview that rules my culture. How could I have missed this point? To be forced to adjust to a worldview that one does not have in one's blood is like walking a tightrope twisted from a set of rules that one has to learn by heart. I suspect that hers is a situation that feels all too familiar to many who, for one reason or another, do not fit in.

As this tale continued to live with me, I had come to wonder whether there was a message in it for me. Maybe this *is* the realization that was awaiting me all those years that I, too, don't fully belong in the culture that has nurtured me. If so, it is an epiphany that comes at the end of a long journey which has awakened me to the understanding that my mythology is more than a two dimensional description of warring worldviews, it is a lived reality filled with pain and anger that continues to affect our world today.

While I have explored this tale with my grown-up understanding, I have also tried to pay attention to the wonder of the child on whom it exerted such a strong attraction.

Menstrual Symbolism

What has this tale got to do with menstruation? The *thurs* is the key. We have explored the *thurs's* relationship with women, first through the rune poems in which the *thurs* is said to cause their sickness and be their torment, and then we saw that Skírnir, emissary of the fertility god Freyr, threatened to carve the *thurs*-rune for Gerd and, thereby, put a spell on her which would have her endure an eternal, hellish cohabitation with a three-headed giant (Chapters 2 & 5). *Gerd*, you remember, is "she who is enclosed." In this tale, the queen is held prisoner in an isolated house, which calls to mind our foremothers' menstrual seclusion apart from the mundane life of family and household chores. During her ordeal, the queen is indeed relieved of her motherly duties and, most likely, of her wifely duties as well as she seems to have become estranged from the king.

As I see it, the queen is living the threats that Skírnir poured out to Gerd.

The tale emphasizes the two poles of woman, the nurturing mother and loving wife on the one hand and the shrew on the other. These opposites may have been linked to the full moon, when ovulation was likely to occur and woman was sexually receptive to her mate, and the new moon, hidden behind a black veil on the evening sky, when she was likely to be menstruating.[2] We note that the queen went through a certain blackness before she landed by the three-headed *thurs* who, I imagine, represents the energies awakened by the dark phase of the moon. In a sense the queen manifests the opposites in nature that we saw presented at the opening of "The Farmer at Fossvellir," the milk ewes attended to by the farmer's daughter and the uncultivated heath with its cascading waterfall where rock giants had their abode (Chapter 7). On the one hand is the domesticated nature that shines through the agreeable demeanor of the princess-wife, who wields no self-determination, and the raw power that manifests in the giantess on the other. The son points the way out of these clashing manifestations of feminine nature, the story seems to suggest. It is the queen's love for her son that helps her transcend the dilemma in which she is caught. Her love for him inspires in her a faith that gives her the courage to act. In this she is very different from Katla who relied on her husband Már to think and act for her (Chapter 5).

The Inner Kingdom

In the introduction to the fairy tales in his collection, Jón Árnason comments that at first sight it might seem that these were foreign

---

2   According to Chris Knight an experiment with light as "an artificial simulation of the effects of the full moon..." suggests "that under ideal conditions, ovulation should occur at full moon, menstruation at new" (p. 251. Ref. to Dewan *et al.* 1978: 582).

tales, as there had never been a king and a queen in their kingdom in Iceland. He ascertains that these tales are nonetheless the product of the Icelandic people's poetic fantasy and not at all translations from foreign stories. This does not mean that Icelanders had never heard of kings and queens. The first official settlers in Iceland were Norsemen who, in the 9th century, fled the tyranny of king Harald Fairhair and would thus have had first-hand knowledge of royal power. From the outset, there were strong ties between the two countries, and Icelandic chieftains and poets were frequent guests at the Norwegian court, as is amply described in the old sagas. So Icelanders would have been familiar, albeit vicariously, with courtly life and its intrigues.

In *Ynglinga saga* ("Saga of the Ynglings"), Snorri Sturluson traces the roots of the Norse kings to Odin and the heathen gods whom he treats as mortal men with superhuman powers who came from Asia to settle in the North. So outstanding were they that they were thought to be more like gods than men. The idea was that these larger-than-life humans had been elevated to the ranks of divinity after their death. This was a device[3] frequently used by Christian authors when writing about the heathen religion which, as Snorri explains, was based on the ancestors' misconception: "They understood everything in an earthly sense for they were not graced with spiritual wisdom. They thought that everything was made of some matter."[4] In *Völsunga saga* ("Saga of the Völsungs"), the genealogy of Sigurd "the dragon slayer" is in like manner traced to Odin. And so were kings and queens in fairy tales seen as having mythological roots. Thus, the name of king Sigurd in "The Giantess on the Stoneboat" suggests his descendency from the legendary hero, and ultimately from Odin. It is a tale that gives us an insight into the mutual evolution of the religion and the culture.

---

3   *Euhemerism,* so called after the historian Euhemeros from Messina who introduced this theory around three centuries before Christ.

4   "Prologus," ch. 2.

The bisexual origin of the species is brought to the fore in the Stone Age sister-brother pair who are seen as evil but turn out to be a transforming evolutionary force. In wordless unison, they do what is needed to elevate the royal couple to a more mature stage. They seem to personify the cooperating, harmonious unity for which we aim as fully conscious beings. This unity the culture saw manifest in Christ as King who unified in himself feminine and masculine nature. And so it seems to me that "The Giantess on the Stoneboat" describes an evolutionary stage from hero consciousness toward Christ consciousness, at the heart of which is altruistic love. For the sake of love for her son, the queen is prepared to surrender herself to the *thurs* who is but a personification of the wild phallic power of her flow. Once upon a time it would have been the natural course of events for a woman to let herself be carried away beyond the confines of the ego where the creative wellspring lies, like did Freyja and the *völvas*. But, due to the projection of evil on woman's menstrual nature, this has become an odious act, hence the uncomely image of the instinct that pulls at her.

As in Katla's case, it is the shadow side of the queen that takes the initiative in bringing transformation about. In both tales, love is a governing factor. In "Katla's Dream" it is conjugal love; in this tale, it is motherly love. The procedure is very different from that of the solar-hero where possession and power appear to be the prime motive for crossing boundaries. Odin's theft of the mead of poetry from Gunnlöd and Skírnir's coercion of Gerd in the service of Freyr's amorous desire are cases in point (Chapters 4 & 5). The former proceeded with trickery and deceit to obtain the booty he desired, while the latter used threats and destructive magic to extort Gerd's consent to surrender herself to Freyr.

The stereotyped role casting in the tales on which we have fed from early childhood affects the way we see ourselves and our world and contributes to maintaining the discrimination between the sexes that we live by. To a child, it will not be immediately apparent that, in a fairy tale, king and queen stand for opposite energies in our make-up. A grown-up may still be hooked by the ingrown assumption that the king is a man and the queen a woman while, symbolically speaking, they represent active and outgoing energies on the one hand and receptive and introverted on the other. The former tends toward differentiation, the latter toward unification. Both are equally important. The king's rank as a ruling principle reflects the status held in our culture by the rational or discriminating mind. As we become increasingly aware that humanity has evolved from a common source, the vital importance of the queen's role is coming to the fore. In order to function as balanced individuals, we need to maintain a harmonious royal couple of equal stature within.

"The Giantess on the Stoneboat" is no exception to stereotyped role casting. The opening line leaves us in no doubt as to who is the star of the tale. *Sigurd*, "he who has victory," is the only personage with a name. This name, as we have seen, hints at his descent from Sigurd "the dragon-slayer," Odin's protégé and the most celebrated solar-hero of all times. The stormy relationship between Sigurd and the Valkyrie Brynhild, as described in the poems of the *Edda* and in *Völsunga saga* ("Saga of the Völsungs"), led to his death and the Valkyrie's suicide (see Page 94). It seems like our tale shows an attempt to progress beyond the fatal relationship between the hero and the belligerent, unyielding Valkyrie.

Mythological Background

As in previous tales, mythological themes inform this story. Behind the two kingdoms we detect the two families of gods, the Vanir venerated by peaceful cultivators of the earth and the heroic Æsir whose main object was conquest of nature and land. In the tale, descendants of these two clans of gods who in the mists of legend were on tense and unfriendly terms, become unified through marriage. The opposite worldviews come together in the son, who incarnates hope for a more peaceful world. That hope, the story may seem to suggest, hinges on woman's separation from the *thurs*, her lunar "other." What seems to have been at stake in the Æsir-religion was to divorce women from their moon god and menstrual power and usurp their divine-creative source in the service of the ruling masculine. But as cyclicity is inherent in a woman's encounter with the *thurs*, we can play with the idea that the queen will be able to draw on her experience and engage this force on a higher level next time around.

The word *Vanir* implies "impotence." The heroic virility manifested in the Æsir-*conquistadors* is lacking in the Vanir. This is emphasized by the predicament of the king, father of the princess-bride, who is unwell and needs Sigurd's help to rule his kingdom. In my child's mind, this immediately raised the question about the constitution of Sigurd's father who is old and decrepit. I never saw any logic in Sigurd's compliance with his father-in-law's wishes. This was a hurdle that cast a shadow on his splendor. How could he just let his own father die without so much as wanting to take leave of him? His contract with his father-in-law did not make any sense to me as there was no visible progress in the king's situation during his stay. His state was seemingly unchanged when Sigurd left. To the grown-up, it is clear that the story is not at all concerned about the fate of that foreign country whose subjects seem to be left to their own devices after Sigurd's departure. It is understood that Sigurd will succeed his father to the throne and carry his banner forth. The sole purpose of this setup is to allow Sigurd to find a wife who infuses his father's kingdom with new blood. Significantly, it is the transforming effect of the queen's *blood* that is at the heart of this tale. There is no mention of a mother or a wife in that foreign kingdom, and again we are reminded of the absence in the myths of the mother of Freyja, daughter of the Vanir-god of fertility, Njord. This absence alludes to the princess's kinship with

Freyja, although on the surface she shows little resemblance with the strong and independent goddess.

Njord's name is etymologically identical to that of a Germanic goddess, *Nerthus*, who according to the Roman historian Tacitus (56-117) was venerated as *Terra mater* ("Mother Earth") on a Danish island in the first century CE. Goddess Nerthus disappeared from the scene and was replaced by Njord, whose name can be traced to places and myths from the latter part of the heathen period. Looking for an explanation of the change of sex, some suggest that in the Nerthus-religion, both a masculine and a feminine deity were venerated as was the case with the twins Freyja and Freyr, children of Njord. Others have claimed that it was a question of one bisexual deity.[5] This background throws light on the sister-brother pair in the tale with which the princess is confronted as she is pulled back to her primitive Stone Age origin on the journey to radical transformation and queenship.

In the spirit of the heroic Æsir, Sigurd's father sends his son out into the world on a wooing journey. The marriage is brought about by a mutual and civilized agreement. This is a far cry from Skírnir's brutal proceedings in extorting Gerd's acceptance of Freyr's proposal. One cannot help but suspect that through the struggle between Freyr (or his emissary) and Gerd, who was a giant maiden, echoes Njord's all but forgotten usurpation of Nerthus' role. Gerd betrays no signs of being a prisoner of her "enclosure" in the giant world, quite the contrary. You will remember that she was enclosed by a wall of fire and a wooden fence to boot, with two ferocious dogs guarding the gate. When Skírnir tries to buy her into surrendering herself to Freyr with gold apples and gold rings, she tells him that there is no shortage of gold at her father's in whose riches she shares. *Skírnismál* ("Lay of Skírnir") thus throws an interesting light on the queen's imprisonment in an isolated house in the giant world.

---

5   Simek, p. 180.

Like an inexplicable mystery, the image of a small *white* house on extensive green fields is deeply engrained in me. I don't know where it came from, but it feels like it has been there always. As I stay with the image and allow it to bring buried feelings to the surface, it occurs to me that it may have come from a compensatory dream, impressed on the child's mind in response to the scary drawing that accompanies the tale. In it, the white-clad queen stands like a helpless little girl on board the boat that comes sailing out of the blackness toward the huge triple-headed giant, whose hungry look and grinning mouths must have inspired terror in me. The giant sits on a stone cube, resting his hands on his knees, leaning forward, as if eagerly awaiting his prey. I could visualize how he lifted her from the boat and put her on his knee...but that was as far as my imagination would take me. I would like to believe that the unconscious sent me the image of the little white house on green fields to counter the distorted fantasy that inspired the making of the monster and its lurid intention.

It was Freyr's overwhelming infatuation with Gerd that prompted Skírnir's mission that led to her consent to indulge Freyr's desire in a grove called Barri.[6] We eventually learn that she became his wife and the mother of his son. In our tale, Sigurd's queen is faced with a three-headed *thurs*, who immediately wants to sleep with her. There appears to be a deep tie between the "Giantess on the Stoneboat" and *Skírnismál* ("Lay of Skírnir"). When Gerd caught Freyr's eye as he sat on Odin's throne, he identified her with the sun. In the mythology, however, it is Freyr who is identified with the sun as is borne out by his attribute, a golden boar called *Gullinbursti* that lit the skies with its "golden bristles."[7] Yet the sun is a feminine entity

---

6   The name has been associated with *barr* as "needles of an evergreen" or (Old Norse) "grain," which seems less likely as it is a grove (Simek, 32).

7   At one time Freyja, too, was associated with the pig for one of her cognomens was *Sýr* which means "sow."

in the language, myth, and minds of the Germanic peoples. The kinship between the desirous nature of the god, as described in the poem, and that of the *thurs* in our tale suggests that before he was adopted into the pantheon of the Æsir, Freyr was a *thurs*. The poem, it seems to me, describes his take-over of the solar power, and the sovereignty that comes with it, previously assigned to his sister and feminine counterpart. In fact, Hilda Ellis Davidson claims that "Gerd is one of the names of the goddess Freyja."[8] This makes sense, that Gerd represented the menstrual aspect of the goddess of love and fertility. And so it is Love, the love of her son that lights the way for the queen through her transformation in her seclusion in the giant world.

For patriarchal culture, it seems to have been of vital importance that the solar power be assigned to a male god. On the Kabbalistic Tree of Life, the sun is assigned the central place, Tiferet or Beauty, and is associated with the heart chakra where the upper and lower realms come together. In that system of thought it is the place of the Son, the sacrificed god. In our tale, the one who is sacrificed is the giantess. Her body, torn apart by wild beasts, evokes the sacrifice of Ymir in the *Gap of Ginnungar* by Odin and his brothers (see Chapter 4). Let us look at this tale. Where is the source of life? Is it not with the giantess who drives the transformation that is called for in a stagnated world? The *thurs* is her servant. He feeds her. She takes the initiative.

Why, my child-self would ask herself in wonder, did the *thurs* not simply have his way with the queen? After all, he was a giant and she just a young girl. It seemed to me natural that the stronger get what they set out to obtain. The outcome of *Skírnismál* and that of Odin's commerce with Gunnlöd would have made more sense to me then. But the *thurs* proceeds in a different manner. He neither forces himself

8   P. 177.

on the queen nor does he rob her. He pays her a visit from time to time (let's presume for argument's sake that he looked in on her once a month!) and keeps her in suspension until a creative solution to her dilemma emerges into the light of her consciousness. She realizes that struggling does not get her anywhere and that redeeming idea is accompanied by surrender and faith. The *thurs* becomes the queen's ally, guiding her towards mature resourcefulness and self-reliance. Where the gods (Odin and Skírnir on Freyr's behalf) diminish feminine power, the *thurs* supports its evolution, and brings about transformation in the masculine and the collective over which it believes itself to be the master.

Giantess as Guardian of Secret

As explained before, the *thurs*-rune that Skírnir threatened to carve for Gerd with devastating consequences, refers to the letter þ, which is named *thorn* and is in actuality the depiction of a thorn on a rose stalk (Þ). The Old Icelandic rune poem throws an interesting light on the *thurs's* paradoxical relationship with the queen:

> *Thurs* is women's torment
> and inhabitant of rocks
> and husband of *vardrún.*
> Saturnus   king (*thengill*).

According to the Icelandic dictionary, *vardrún* denotes a "giantess." *Vard-* means "guard" and *rún* (rune) is a "secret." What I read into this is that *vardrún* is simultaneously the guardian of a secret and a secret guardian. This was particularly clear in "Katla's Dream" (Chapter 5) where Alvör's maneuverings prevented the collective from becoming cut off from its heritage and natural origin and brought about transformation toward reconciliation and peace in a world governed by the sword. The giantess in our story works toward a similar purpose. The royal couple has to face and find grounding in their natural origin in order to grow up and fulfill their roles with wisdom. In my mind, *vardrún* is a guardian and a guide who works in mysterious ways toward the good of all.

In our tale, the *thurs* is the giantess' brother. The rune poem rhymes with what Snorri says in *Ynglinga saga* ("Saga of the Ynglings"), that before Njord joined the ranks of the Æsir, he had been married to his sister, for such was the law with the Vanir.[9] The boundaries between the brother-sister pair are fluid, their interaction is without words as if they share one mind. Saturn, a Roman fertility god whose reign was the Golden Age of early humanity, is the key to the meaning of *thurs*. As a fertility god, Saturn was in one sense the Reaper and personification of Time, but he was also *thengill*, the meaning of which is "king" and, according to the origin of the word, "he who promotes growth and well-being amongst his subjects."[10] Accordingly, *thurs* is a personification for the fertility cycle and the growth that inheres in death. It is to this ground that menstruation ties woman, a thread of red-gold, which links her vulva to the source of life and death through generations gone by and to those to come.

The *thurs* in our tale has little in common with Snorri Sturluson's inspired description of Saturn whom he credits with superhuman strength, beauty, and innovative wisdom. He possessed the gift of prophecy and discovered bog iron ore in the earth from which he made gold. His was a time of wealth and prosperity. Eventually, Saturn's son, Jupiter, had his father castrated. Saturn then fled to Italy where he took the name Njord and taught the Romans to plow the earth and cultivate vineyards.[11] The rune poem traces the roots of the *thurs* to the cave-dweller in us and the primitive belief that woman gained access to a secret (rune) through her intimate relationship with the *thurs*. Hence the *thurs*-maiden was a sought after treasure as symbolized by Freyja's daughter *Hnoss* ("treasure") begotten by

---

9   Ch. 4.

10   Blöndal, p. 1175.

11   "Prologus," chs. 5 & 7.

"wild" *Od*, who by virtue of his name personified "poetry," a source that lay outside the confines of the conscious ego and contained the key to the ultimate secret of being. This is the matrilineal descent of the princess in our tale. She is the "treasure" that Sigurd's father had his eye on, a wife who would provide fertile soil for his son's nobility to attain full flower. The parallel Snorri draws between Saturn and Njord leads to the sister-brother pair Nerthus / Njord which seems to inform "The Giantess on the Stoneboat."

We have already seen that in Celtic lore the Cup was the attribute of the Goddess of the Land, Lady Sovereignty (see Page 112). A new king wed himself to the goddess by drinking from a cup offered him by her mortal representative. In "The Giantess on the Stoneboat," this archaic custom has become a mere figure of speech. Sigurd "drank his wedding to the princess" but the land that she represents is of no consequence in the tale. Sigurd is going to make her the queen of *his* kingdom. But while the bride's role as Sovereignty may have fallen into disuse and been forgotten, the repressed reality swells beneath the surface.

Unlike Freyja and unlike Gerd, the princess does not wield sovereignty over herself. It is not she but her father who decides whether or whom she marries. And, even as she is a married woman and a mother, she still lives like a child within the protecting walls of her father's palace. We can surmise that her father's reluctance to let go of his princess-daughter has delayed her growing-up process. Only when she is outside the boundaries of patriarchal order and in the natural domain of the mother can her initiation commence. She is playing with her son on the ship's deck as a girl would with a doll when a giantess, seemingly from the Stone Age, pops up from the unconscious and literally turns her inside out.

The Princess's Shadow Side Comes to the Fore

Sigurd's reaction to the change in his wife "who had never before spoken a cross word to him," intimates that, like Thorunn Sigurdardottir in "The 'Hidden Woman' in Hafnanúpur" and other paragons of ideal behavior held up to young girls, she had been brought up to be well-behaved and agreeable. Once her guard is down, repressed anger breaks forth like an ice-bound river in spring. No longer a passive girl, she takes the initiative to awaken Sigurd and takes him to task. Even if impetuous, there is no denying the truth in her words. Sigurd is not living up to his name. He has neglected the hero's ultimate duty of vigilance. He has been caught off-guard. Paradoxically, it is this breach of the heroic code that leads to a radical transformation.

Sigurd and his wife betray signs of immaturity while they are on the threshold of assuming collective responsibility. Their growing-up process has a universal appeal in that it is every individual's ultimate duty to contribute to the good of all. That they lose wind and become adrift in dead calm implies stagnation. This is when a primal force stirs in the psyche, proving the dictum that "every paradise has its serpent." The giantess raises havoc in the young couple's blissful world but, significantly, becomes the driving force in their maturation process. We can only speculate how far Sigurd would have gotten with the obedient and agreeable princess-wife he set out with by his side.

The Chess Players' Role

The game of chess is an ingenious story telling device that mirrors the tale in a nutshell. Like the game, the story revolves around the battle between black and white, between the light and the dark forces. In chess, white has the first move. This comports with the heroic worldview wherein the solar-hero journeys to another world to win "the treasure hard to obtain." Likewise, Sigurd travels outside the boundaries of his known world to seek his bride. Black's countermove, in the guise of the underworld powers, thwarts a smooth and easy conquest and thereby initiates his real maturation process through the transformation of his feminine counterpart. The queen is unquestionably the most powerful piece on the chess board, and the piece that has the greatest mobility. In the tale, this aptitude is reflected in the queen's ability to move both horizontally and vertically. She is in direct communion with another world, while the chess players witness the events from outside. One of them is 18, the other 19. I cannot help but wonder why the age of those boys is so specified. It is a curious synchronicity that in the system of tarot, the Moon is Major Arcana card number 18 and the Sun number 19 (see images).

The progression from 18 to 19, from Moon to Sun, would mean that something stirring in the unconscious is revealed to consciousness (see Page 47 for interpretation of the Moon card). This is in fact the chess players' role in the tale. They witness what is hidden inside the queen's chamber (the moon within the sun!) and reveal it to the king. But the question that needs to be asked is, from what premise do they interpret what they see?

The intrusion of the giantess echoes the mythological theme illustrated in *Völuspá* ("Prophecy of the Seeress") in which the *völva* describes the golden age at Idavellir when Odin and his brothers have completed the creation of their splendid world. In carefree joy, the Æsir are sitting over a game of chess in the fields when three powerful *"thursa meyjar"* (maidens who consort with *thurses*) come from the giant world and put an end to their sense of omnipotence and shadowless existence. With that scene of cloudless innocence in mind, the Sun card could be seen as an optimistic beginning of a new cycle. A joyous child leaves an enclosed garden, ready to embrace a bright new world.

THE MOON

THE SUN

If the giantess in the tale is the *Vardrún* of the rune poem discussed above, then what secret does she guard? Does the tale give us a clue? Could it be the essence of the true self symbolized by the queen in her white underwear and stripped of the trappings of her role? Is not our role a mask behind which we not only hide our primitive origin but which also limits our sphere of action and development? What strikes me is that this unshapely mass of flesh is accompanied by Spirit in the guise of fair and propitious wind. Perhaps Vardrún is the "World Soul" who animates Creation and drives man's evolution toward the intended goal. The giantess is undeniably the driving force in this tale, and it is she who reveals the queen's true self to us as a desirable goal.

The brother-sister pair is observed by the chess players through a slit in the wall between their room and that of the queen. Of the same significance is the slit in the roof through which the stable boy in "The Witch's Ride" (Chapter 6) observes the commerce between Satan and the pastors' wives. This imagery is a veiled reference to the female orifice, the vulva, as a gate leading into a mysterious realm of superhuman wisdom and power. This is where the secret lies hidden.

Menstruant as Mother

The game of chess which takes place on a board marked with distinct squares and according to specific rules, is in contrast to the crucible of the unconscious where boundaries are unclear and one thing metamorphoses into another. The queen's yawning indicates numbness and lack of concentration. As we later learn when the queen tells her story, she is suspended between worlds. Her energy is trapped in an inner conflict, which causes absent-mindedness and lack of feeling in her daily life at the court. She is listless and seemingly in the throes of existential nausea. Could this description fit a woman in disaccord with her feminine nature? We know what she is dealing with: her lunar "other" on whom patriarchal culture has projected a triple-headed monster. As the telluric counterpart of the celestial trinity, the triple-headed *thurs* vies for her soul. The food that the giant brings her points to the unconscious as a nourishing power source and may be an attempt to explain the giant maiden's legendary strength.

The woman, who under those circumstances is unable to impart motherly love to her son, is a repeated theme in fairy tales. In the tale about *Mjadveig Mánadóttir* (her given name refers to mead, or *honey wine*, and her surname means "daughter of the Moon"), the dilemma has been cast in a poem. As the queen in our tale, queen Mjadveig is dispatched into the hands of an ugly giant by a giantess who overtakes her role. Where before flowers had blossomed, cuckoos called and a ram shed its fleece in Mjadveig's hall, now

> "cuckoos do not call,
> flowers do not blossom
> and a ram does not shed its fleece
> and never quiets down the young boy
> who lies in the cradle

and everything seems to be going askew in the kingdom." When the giantess has been subjected to a scornful death, equilibrium is restored and

> "then cuckoos call
> and then flowers blossom
> and then a ram sheds its fleece,
> then stays quiet the young boy
> who lies in the cradle."[12]

---

12   "Mjaðveig Mánadóttir" in Árnason, II.

The Nanny and Her Vision

The nanny is played against the giantess. The image of her sitting with the prince in her lap by a burning light has a saintly aura. The queen is suspended between the poles of light and darkness. The motherly love is strong, and it is bright and beautiful but her religious impulse (in the sense of linking back to the source) pulls at her, and it is illegitimate, dark, and scary. While woman is tied to Saturnian soil, she is not fit to be the mother of a son. This is the moral of the story. She is to break with her past and devote herself wholly to the sacred role of raising her son. In this lies her redemption.

Although it is Sigurd who cuts the cord between the queen and the *thurs*, and thereby reclaims his wife, it is the nanny who with her insight and courage has prepared the case for him. She is scared but she does not shy away from her experience and tries to decipher its meaning. The thrice-repeated vision denotes an urgent attempt on behalf of the unconscious to convey its message to the one-sided conscious mind. Her attitude exemplifies how important it is to listen to the inner voice, whether it speaks to us in dreams or visions. We see how a suspicion is awakened and how it gradually leads to an understanding and transformation. We also see that the resolution of a problem depends on the cooperation of feminine and masculine traits. The nanny personifies insight, a trait associated with feminine nature. She receives messages from another dimension and allows them to brew within her before she mediates them to the king, who with his drawn sword, stands for the clarity of the rational mind.

The King's Role

It is the king who separates the essence from the husk when he recognizes his wife in her underwear. Thereby he passes the ultimate test of differentiating the true from the false. The king's role and status emphasize the prominence of the rational mind over and above natural insight and wisdom. At the same time, the tale reveals that without the latter the king would not have reached this apex, thus confirming the value of feminine nature. Still, the tale ranks it considerably lower on the scale of values than that of the masculine. The reward reaped by the nanny, who may well be the hero of this tale, consists in landing a wealthy and powerful husband and a generous dowry.

Because the roles in these stories are gender-bound, they contribute to maintaining stereotypes, which inevitably clash with our experience of ourselves, for as individuals we are endowed with traits that are associated with feminine nature and masculine discrimination, although the tendency toward one or the other may differ from one person to the next. The twin theme of the underworldy sister-brother pair that underlies this tale points to an egalitarian origin. It is toward this inborn balance of the opposites that we aim, within and without.

Maturation implies cultivating traits, which are underdeveloped in our personality so that we can become whole. As conscious beings we need to control our instincts and feelings but it is also vital that we be in touch with and establish a positive relationship with these same powers. The king valiantly cuts the chain that binds his wife to her origin. The liberation is double-edged. It is positive in that the woman needs to encounter this inner power consciously and on her own terms, but not by compulsion. It is negative in that the attitude to the female power source presented in the tale is hostile. The king's action seemingly aims at separating the queen from her primitive origin once and for all. But do we not detect a resistance on the part of those who span this tale to collude with patriarchy's wishful thinking? Does the indefinite fate of the giant not imply their knowledge that as surely as the moon continues its cycle through four phases, the *thurs* will return and visit the woman when the moon's luminous body disappears from the sky?

The Giantess's Fate

The fate of the ungracious queen is intended as a deterrent for young girls. Women are to be obedient, gentle, and polite, but not to behave like giantesses. They are not to say what they think, not to raise their voice, not to take the initiative in their relationship with men, but rather be affable and submissive wives. To protect himself from the giantess' evil eye, the king had a hood pulled over her head before she was stoned to death and then torn apart by unbroken colts, which no doubt were meant to mirror her wild nature. This is the retributive punishment of fairytales with which patriarchy washes its hands of its violence against feminine nature.

When the queen is released, she assumes her noble role and is well-liked by all. This is presented as a worthy goal to young girls who all dream of becoming queens! Yet the path leading to this desirable finale is not only depicted as thorny, but the sexual-creative pull of the unconscious is demonized to such an extent that few are likely to feel tempted to walk this way of their own accord. Young women are to learn their lesson by way of indoctrination. The queen's feat consists in resisting the *thurs's* amorous advances. And the *thurs*, in spite of his superhuman power, does not take her by force but keeps her in suspension until the solution emerges into the light of her consciousness. It is not for nothing that Saturn, with whom the *thurs* is identified in the rune poem quoted above, is rumored to be a "strict task master!"

The conclusion of the tale sums up its core message: to be likeable is a female virtue of the highest rank. The urge to please that is instilled in young females prevents them from knowing and showing their true selves.

9
"The Outcast"

from *Icelandic Folk and Fairy Tales*, II
collected by Jón Árnason

The storyteller's switching from the past to the present
tense in moments of tension has been left intact.

Once upon a time there was an old couple who lived in a cottage
far away from any other human habitation. They had three
daughters, Ingibjörg, Sigridur, and Helga. The first two were
older than Helga, and they were held in far higher regard than the
youngest, even though they were neither better than nor as gifted
as she. Helga was not trusted with anything for supposedly she was
capable of nothing.

Thus it came about, when one day the fire went out in the cottage, that one of the older sisters was asked to fetch fire. She set out on her mission, and when she passed by a mound on her way, she heard someone say inside: "Do you want to have me as your friend or foe?" She imagined that these words were meant for her and said that she did not care. She proceeded till she came to a cave. Here there was no shortage of fire, for meat was cooking in a kettle and there was flatbread in a tray nearby. The girl did not see any person nor was there any sign of life. Being hungry she fanned up the fire under the kettle and baked the cakes, one for herself, and that one she made right, but the others she burned and made them inedible. She then ate the food. But when she has finished her meal, an awfully big dog comes and fawns upon her. She hits it and tries to chase it away. The dog then becomes angry and bites off one of her hands. At that she becomes so terrified that she runs away without taking the fire. She makes it back home and describes her tribulations to the wonder-struck household.

Athough such a journey was considered terribly risky, the other favorite was asked to go. They all feared that the youngest daughter would use the opportunity to run away, as she would, by no means, be leaving a haven. She was, however, useful to wait on the rabble. This one went through the same experience as her sister before, except the dog bit the nose off of her. She too returned without bringing her mission to a successful end.

The third was then ordered to pick up and go. She did as she was told. She came to the mound and was asked the same question as the others. She responded that it was a saying that nothing was so wretched that it was not better to have it as friend than foe and she would be glad to have an ally in whomever was asking. She then proceeded till she came to the cave. Everything was as when her sisters arrived, but she was in every way more considerate. She cooked the meat and baked the cakes with thorough care, but she did not take any food although she had not eaten for a long time and was overcome by fatigue. Nor did she take the fire, for she wanted the permission of whomever was master of the place. She therefore decided to stay the night, even if it felt scary.

When she is looking for a place to lie down, a thundering noise rips through the cave and in comes a loathsome giant with a huge dog. She became terrified but felt somewhat reassured when the giant addressed her with these gentle words: "You have attended well and faithfully to what needed to be done and therefore you shall be rewarded for your work and have supper with me. Afterwards you may choose whether to sleep with the dog in its lair or share my bed." When he had spoken those words, she took a bit of food and then lay down in the dog's lair, for although the dog seemed dreadful it felt like a better choice than sleeping with the giant. When she had lain there for a while, a formidable quake shook the cave. She became beside herself with fear and terror but to her consolation the giant called out to her and said: "If you are afraid, Helga 'the old man's daughter,' you are welcome to creep upon the platform by my bed." And so she did. There followed another and much stronger quake. He now invited her to sit on his bed, and she accepted. At the third and by far the strongest quake, she was invited to lie down by his feet, and when the fourth almost ripped the cave asunder, she picked herself up and lay down between him and the wall. At that, the giant shed his shape and by her side was a handsome prince. Her first reaction was to light a fire and burn the slough he had shed. He thanked her passionately for having freed him, and they slept for the rest of the night.

When morning came, he told her that he was a prince who had been bewitched and that he would come for her later if she agreed, and she for her part was not unwilling to betroth herself to him. He then gave her a gown, a true treasure, and told her to wear it next to her, beneath the rags, so no one could see it. He also gave her a chest filled with jewels and riches. He said that those things she could show but warned her that they would be taken away from her.

When she was ready to leave, the dog came and reached its right forepaw toward her. She took it and found that it held a large gold ring which she accepted. She then set out home although she was deeply sad to part from the prince. She arrived home safely with the fire, but when the household discovered the chest and treasures, they broke out in jubilation, and she was immediately dispossessed of everything they knew she had brought with her. Two sets of women's clothing had also been in the chest and the elder sisters took one each, so nothing remained for Helga except the gown that no one, but she alone, knew about.

Time passed and nothing changed in the cottage and nothing noteworthy happened, until one day a beautiful and well-equipped ship is seen sailing toward land. The old man goes down to shore to spy on who was in charge of the ship, but he did not know the man. The two talked for a while, and the stranger asked how many they were on the farm and how many children he had. The old man said they were five and that he had two daughters. The stranger asked to see his daughters. The old man gladly assented and went to fetch the two older ones. They came decked up in the clothes they had taken from their sister. The stranger said he found them quite good looking but why, he wanted to know, did one have her hand tucked in her bosom and the other her nose covered with a scarf? The sisters were compelled to expose themselves, and the stranger felt that their charm was greatly diminished, but he could not get them to disclose how this had come about. He asked whether it was absolutely certain that the old man did not have other daughters. The old man steadfastly refused, but when the stranger questioned him more closely, he admitted that he had one wretch but said that he did not know for sure whether she was a human or a beast. The stranger was eager to see her and the old man went to fetch Helga. She was in her rags, but when the stranger and she had found each other, he rips her rags off of her and she stood there in her dazzling gown that far outshone the ones that her sisters wore.

The stranger then turned around and rebuked the father and the sisters for their treatment of Helga. He dispossessed the sisters of their finery, making it clear that it was not theirs, and threw Helga's rags at them. He then made the old man and his two daughters leave the ship and sailed with Helga to the kingdom he was to inherit. He married Helga, and they loved each other well for a long time.

INTERPRETATION

The Way of the Feminine

I have suggested that the myth about Freyja's acquisition of Brísingamen reflected a ritual reenactment of the original episode, the first menstrual flow as experienced and envisioned by our ancestresses at the dawn of day (Chapter 1). We all know by now that she was rumored to have slept with four dwarfs in a cave, one night with each, in return for her gold necklace which is also referred to as a gold ring. I also suggested that the image of the necklace was derived from an eclipse of the sun in accordance with the Hermetic dictum "as above, so below," depicting the blood *lacing* the *neck* of her womb. At the outset, I explained that *Brísinga-men* is a compound word meaning "fire" and "moon." The object of Helga's quest is fire and, as I will argue later, her gold ring and the fire are seemingly interchangeable. The reason the fire has gone out in the cottage, I venture, is that the ritual practiced by our foremothers has been forgotten and with it the sense of the sacred attached to the incipient movement of evolution associated with the first flow.

What Helga finds in the cave is genuine love, love that looks beyond appearances. By overcoming her fear and disgust of the giant and accepting his offer to crawl into bed with him, Helga reclaims the goddess's lost jewel. It is the essence that matters, not the husk.

This is the wisdom that the tale imparts. We find the theme repeated in the dazzling gown that Helga wears beneath her rags. Not before we can love that which we fear and despise in ourselves, can we become whole and the world a more peaceful place.

In my entry on "Menstruation" in *The Book of Symbols: Reflections on Archetypal Images*, I wrote: "The chord struck at a girl's first flow reverberates through her subsequent cycles. It can become her key to the music of being or throw her into discord with her own self."[1] As I see it, "The Outcast" reflects an attempt to regain a state of natural harmony that woman senses in the depths of her being. The older sisters personify the legendary irascibility that tends to grip women around the time of menstruation and *Helga*, whose name means "holy, whole, wholesome," points the way towards restoration of the desired state.

The Alchemy Inherent in the Menstrual Cycle

The isolated cottage under the rulership of the "old man" in the tale points to a narrow and outworn worldview. Without fire, it is a place of sterility and stagnation. Renewal is called for. In traditional society, every time something new comes into being, there is a creation myth behind it. Creation is repeated in some form. The same is true of the individual psyche as alchemical symbolism suggests. We go through the phase of *nigredo* as we are pulled into a state of blackness and dissolution through which we have to make our way without familiar guideposts, until the sun eventually rises again and lights up a new world. It is new because we see it in a different light. A radical transformation has taken place within us, which infuses us with life and prompts us to engage the world in a fresh way. Regression precedes progression to a more mature worldview. In a

---

1   P. 402.

sense we are pulled back to the zero-point of the Fool (see image in Chapter 4). The Fool's "dazzling white inner robe," said to represent "the light of perfect wisdom," calls to mind the gown that Helga wears beneath her rags.[2]

With the enticing character of the Fool in mind, let us go back to the Norse creation myth discussed in Chapter 4. Recall that sparks of fire and blasts of rime came together in the Gap of *Ginnungar* ("fools") and from the drip engendered by the merging of the opposites life was kindled in the guise of *Ymir* whose name means "twin." I suggested that, at this moment, woman awakened to the sense of an "other" within who was not she, but who was intimately related to her. And she experienced this "other" as a mystery, a divine being who came from outside of her and visited her in dreams and visions, frequently in different guises, for this inner self was a mirror image reflected to her solar consciousness by her lunar unconscious, emphasizing aspects of herself with which she needed to become acquainted. In general terms, this is how the communion between self and "other" still unfolds. The fact that the moon is reborn every month, as is the menstruating woman, would have contributed to the idea of multiple "lovers" as we see reflected in Skadi's cognomen "chaste bride of gods" (Page 89). This too, I imagine, would have brought upon Freyja the reputation of a "whore."

Another name for Ymir was *Aurgelmir. Aur-* is "mud, mire," but it is also a denomination for money, traced to Lat. *aurum* meaning "red-gold." In modern times, albeit no longer in use, *aur* is a copper red coin, the smallest, indivisible denomination, like the American penny. Mindful of Freyja's tear of red-gold on which we have elaborated in previous chapters, it is tempting to conclude that at the dawn (which by the way is associated with the same color as is borne

---

2   Case, p. 32.

out by its personification, goddess Aurora) of human consciousness a parallel was drawn between *mire* as a metaphor for the earth-goddess's menstrual blood and the bleeding vulva. It would rhyme with the claim that Saturn, whom the rune poem identified with *thurs* as "women's torment" found bog iron ore in the earth from which he made gold (Page 176). The analogy between the female body and the earth that informs mythological thought is rooted in the concept that man[3] is a microcosmic reflection of the macrocosm.

As *aur* refers to both mire and gold, *gelmir* was used in poetic parlance for both "worm" and "hawk," and worm in this case could refer to any creature with that shape, such as a snake or a serpent-like monster.[4] Aurgelmir thus alludes to the oneness that inheres in creation. *Aur* is both the *prima materia* ("raw material") and the end result, the spiritual gold toward which alchemy in its highest aspect aimed. As gold it stands for the potential inherent in the menarcheal girl to be attained through conscious collaboration with her menstrual nature. This was understood by our foremothers who practiced "alchemy" in their bowers and isolated cottages. Maybe the oneness implied by Aurgelmir is nowhere as apparent as when woman as a conscious being is pulled down into her body during her period by the superhuman force of nature. I have elaborated on the snake's relationship with the menstruating womb and in "The Witch's Ride," we saw that Freyja and Frigg both owned a falcon dress. They were thus able to fly. So were the Valkyries who were identified with both the swan and the raven (see Page 53). These images evoke spiritual exuberance with which our foremothers, who were in tune with their lunar nature, were carried up to the heavens by the power of their flow. This soaring exuberance echoes in a poem by a woman poet who calls on the moon to carry her up to

---

3   It is interesting to note that "man" includes woman while the prefix in *w*oman is derived from OE. *wif* = "wife".

4   *Íslensk orðabók,* p. 443; p. 1095.

the clouds so that she can explore new worlds.[5] It is easy to imagine that her ode was inspired by such experience and that its appeal to the masses points to a deeply felt collective reality.

As both a snake and a hawk, *gelmir* calls to mind the dictum "as above, so below." So, too, does the association of the serpent with the "flash of lightening snaking across the sky."[6] Swiftness is a common characteristic of these opposite phenomena. As a metaphor for mire and menstrual blood, *aur* illustrates the dictum "as without, so within." The same principle applies to fire. Fire is the primary source of life and culture, and it is the Eros in the blood that drives us toward the perfected wholeness from which we originated. This was the ultimate goal of the alchemists, their philosophical gold. Fire cleanses and transforms, and transformation is what the greedy materialist household ruled by the "old man" needs. Every step of the way, we are faced with the fact that there is nothing new under the sun!

The Spell in the Garden

As the Bible story and numerous other traditional tales reveal, the female is an initiator. Her blossoming womanhood is the temptation that drives the male to deed. What drives the female, according to Biblical tradition, is evil in the guise of the snake. The Eden story seemingly reflects reversal of values. The curse that the Lord puts on woman implies that pain shall replace pleasure. The enmity God establishes between woman and the serpent indicates that the two were previously on peaceful terms. And, curiously, that the serpent is told it shall crawl on its belly can only mean that originally it had legs and feet with which to walk! Might this be a reference to the

---

5   "Tunglið, tunglið taktu mig / og berðu mig upp til skýja..." by Theodóra Thoroddsen (1863-1954).

6   Charbonneau-Lassey, p. 156.

moon-spirit who was rumored to roam the earth in the guise of a male and deflower young girls at the onset of their menstruation? It would seem that the serpent is a bewitched creature if ever there was one! Thus the serpent is a symbol for something beyond its literal meaning and is, as we know, traditionally associated with the Devil of Christian teachings who also goes by the names of Satan and Lucifer. Archeological research has revealed, as has been repeatedly mentioned, that the serpent was an attribute of the Goddess, associated with the womb and inherent female wisdom. Both phenomena shed their skin and renew themselves, just as the Moon sheds its old self as it disappears into Earth's shadow and is reborn in bright splendor three or four nights later from the veiled cauldron in the evening sky. This eternal cyclicity is reflected in the fairy tale when the giant sloughs off his terrifying shape and transforms into a handsome prince.

The Voice of Nature

The voice in the mound and the unfolding of the story emphasize once again that it is our attitude toward nature that determines whether we experience it as friend or foe. Nature itself is neutral. The same applies to a woman's attitude toward her menstruation as Annette Høst so beautifully illustrates in "Blessed by the Moon." If she fights its untamable power, it becomes a nightmare, or "what has been labelled PMS, the premenstrual syndrome, the horrible monster." But, says Høst, "just because we cannot control the power doesn't mean that we cannot 'ride' its waves and make use of it." She suggests that PMS be replaced with "The Moment of Truth!" If a woman chooses to listen to this power and cooperate with it, she can make creative use of it. Stressing the kinship between her shamanistic work and the power of menstruation and dreamwork, Høst states that the wild power of menstruation speaks from a place of unadulterated truth and that it responds to the woman's attention and curiosity, as do our dreams. Helga's respectful attention to the voice in the mound solicits the alliance of instinct in bringing her quest to a successful end.

The interaction between the dog and the sisters is of interest in this context. In "The Witch's Ride" (Page 129), we saw that the wolf, its wild relative and ancestor, was said to have been the mount of giantesses who fearlessly rode this wild animal power. The Æsir on the other hand were fearful of the wolf as it was prophesied to become Odin's bane and they tricked it into letting itself be bound. This beast of doom was called *Fenrir*, "wolf of the quagmires." The image evokes the fear of being swallowed by the earth, of becoming disintegrated in the grave. The womb which swallows the sperm and tears potential life asunder in menstruation like the wolf its prey and disgorges it in a stream of blood, was most likely seen as a parallel fear-inspiring image. Surprisingly, however, the saliva running from the bound Fenrir's gaping mouth is a river called *Vón*, which means "Hope."[7] It is a name that scholars find perplexing given the river's dangerous source.[8] I venture that Helga's successful mission is a manifestation of that hope.

In spite of the Æsir's effort to prevent the prophecy from coming true, the *völva* announces the pending end of Odin's reign in a thrice-repeated refrain, *Garmur bays in front of Gnipa-cave, the shackles will break and the wolf will run loose*.[9] Although in another source, *Garmur* is said to rank highest among dogs,[10] in *Völuspá* ("Prophecy of the Seeress") it appears to be the wolf. The cave, in front of which the beast is shackled, is held to derive its name from *gnipall* which is a designation for "fire."[11] As opposed to the destruction depicted in

---

7   Snorri Sturluson. "Gylfaginning," ch. 34.

8   Simek, p. 252.

9   *Völuspá* ("Prophecy of the Seeress"), sts. 43, 47, 56.

10   *Grímnismál* ("Lay of Grímnir"), st. 44.

11   Magnússon, p. 263.

the poem, brought about by the gods' fear and deceiving of the wolf, the dog leads the courageous Helga to "the treasure hard to obtain." It is my belief that in Helga we have a trailblazer of the new cycle announced by the *völva* when she sees the green earth rise anew out of the apocalyptic chaos.

The older sisters all but ignore the voice in the mound. We can imagine that they have learned the lesson imprinted on them, not to emulate Eve and listen to their inner voice lest they be led astray and the whole of humanity with them. As an outsider, Helga is an innocent, much like the Fool in Tarot who as number o stands outside the system. She is free of social prejudices, hence she is open to the experiences that come her way. She is the undefended heart. Her father's unkind description of her to the stranger at the end of the tale places her on the fluid boundaries of humanness and nature, of man and beast. She is neither one nor the other, but both. As is emphasized by the meaning of her name, "whole, holy, wholesome," Helga is a unifying symbol.

The Silent Self

In my mind, Helga is the silent self who guides us on our quest for Love and never gives up on us, regardless of the abuse we inflict on her. Like her merciless family in the tale, we may fear to lose her. But like our shadow, Helga is a constant. We can depend on her. Her dazzling gown, hidden under her rags, emphasizes our ignorance of the real and the sacred. Such is pretty much our attitude towards menstruation. Menstruation is every woman's reality, yet it has been an underground issue in our culture. It is woman's hidden secret and her source of power. A woman cannot become whole until she has accepted her underground partner, her shadow. And that implies embracing her body and its mortality. Death resides in the body. Death inheres in nature. It is the fear of death that keeps us in shackles. If we control our fear and dare trust our instincts, we obtain the treasure. This is the truth the story imparts. The mistreatment of Helga by her community reflects the culture's attitude toward the menstrual aspect of feminine nature which it has made an outcast. Yet Helga continues to silently serve us and patiently waits for our eyes to open. A servant in the interest of life, she teaches us by example how to interact with nature, within and without. She is a star that lights the way for us so that we, too, can rise above self-interest and contribute to the healing of the world.

Helga knows that we are not masters in our house and acts accordingly. She is whole in her actions. She accepts but does not take. She is afraid but controls her fear. She is moderate, not greedy like her sisters. And unattached to worldly goods, she takes it lightly that her community robs her of the things she brought back from her journey. The dazzling gown that she wears beneath her rags, unbeknownst to all but herself, is what counts above all. It stands for her sense of self that nobody can take away from her.

The attitude of the elder sisters is testimony to, not only women's alienation from feminine nature, but also their adjustment to the patriarchal mindset. Their lack of reverence, their self-interest, arrogance and greed are reflective of man's self-appointed exploitative lordship over nature and its resources. Clearly the sisters need to be taught a lesson for the paradigm to change. So we have a couple of nightmares to shake things up. The tale can be understood to reveal repressed material that is struggling to reemerge in order to create balance in an aggressive patriarchal culture that has divested feminine nature of its sacredness and healing potency. The three sisters would then represent repeated attempts to arrive at a resolution to a pressing problem. And as is wont in fairy tales, the youngest sibling is the one who brings home the treasure that lies outside the confines of the conscious ego.

Kettle in the Cave

The cave, as the habitat of our ancestors at the dawn of civilization, is the deepest place within, symbolizing our common and humble origin. In this primal sanctuary, food is cooking over fire. In a literal sense, kettle or cauldron is used for cooking raw meat to facilitate its digestion. Metaphorically, it is a vessel in which raw instincts cook over the inner fire until the individual has transformed them into wholesome nourishment, which she or he assimilates and shares in word or deed with the outer world. As a central image, the kettle is symbolic of the alchemical process reflected in the tale. The elder sisters do not pass the giant's test. Their egocentricity is generated by base instincts that need more cooking till they have come to understand that they are not the center of the universe and that their negligence and lack of concern have consequences for the whole of which they are a part.

Dog as Guide

Helga's respectful awe of nature is in contrast to the hubris, violence and betrayal that the typical hero of myth and fairy tales vents on its shadowy inhabitants who are experienced as the enemy. The older sisters meet the dog's friendly greeting with violence and, consequently, come home un-whole (with missing parts!). One loses a hand, the other her nose. Just as we need to access both the right and the left hemispheres of the brain to function holistically, so we need the function of both hands if only to accomplish our daily tasks. The nose signifies sensitivity that the dog possesses to a high degree, enabling it to sniff its way to a goal. This heightened sense of smell civilized man has lost. Helga, who encompasses both the human and the animal, receives a gold ring, symbol of wholeness, from the dog's paw. Due to its extraordinary sensitivity and close relationship with man, many mythologies present the dog as a guide to the other world (see image of "The Fool" and her "guide" in Chapter 4). In our tale, it acts as an intermediary between Helga and the giant / prince. She goes from its lair to the giant's bed, and it is the dog who gives her the ring marking the mutual vow between her and the prince.

In a variation of the tale, the dog's role as Helga's guide is even clearer. When the elder sisters have returned home bitten by the dog and without fire, Helga is dispatched on the quest for fire in a fury. She arrives at a mountain where her sisters had been before, sits down on the same stone to rest as they had, and hears a voice calling from the mountain above her: "Lone dweller in a mountain. Lone dweller in a mountain." Where the elder sisters had replied to this appeal: "Stay the most wretched of men, lone dweller in a mountain" and thereby provoked the dog's ire, Helga responds:

> "Sit the halest of men, lone dweller in a mountain!" Then the big dog comes and fawns upon Helga and allures her into a cave in the mountain. She stays there the night and shares the dog's lair. The dog then sheds its slough which Helga burns in the morning. But instead of a dog a handsome prince is lying by her side in the lair.

The Gold Ring

In the context of *men*struation, the gold ring can be seen as a symbol for woman's betrothal to her feminine nature that is attuned to the moon (*men*) and its cycle. This rhythmic relationship is the ground of her being. The initiation into the mystery of the blood is a precursor to her union with a spouse. Through repeated encounters (here symbolized by the three sisters) with her inhuman "other," i.e. the menstrual flow, which is ruled by nature and hence is uncivilized, woman not only gains awareness of her own essence but also transforms that "other" into the ideal soulmate. This mystery is the seeding place of Love. We saw this in Thorn-Rose whose prince we felt represented this ideal. Whether a princess or a pauper, menstruation is every woman's reality just as we are all equal in the face of death. As Thorn-Rose slept for a hundred years behind the thornhedge before she was touched by the magic spark of love, in this tale "time passed and nothing changed in the cottage and nothing noteworthy happened" until the prince appeared on the scene and immediately saw Helga's dazzling beauty through her rags. The process is a long one. The key to success, the story tells us, is a positive attitude and receptivity towards nature, trust in the rightness of instinct, and restraint of fear.

Curiously, the gold ring is never mentioned again, but immediately after Helga has received it, the story stresses that she gets home safely with the fire, which becomes totally overshadowed by her community's greed. It is as if ring and fire are one and the same. The assimilation between the two phenomena appears to be derived from the flaming solar prominences whirling around the black disk of the moon during an eclipse. What Helga finds in the ancestral cave, the place of humanity's origin, is the moon-spirit to whom she betroths herself. She returns home with love and desire in her blood. This invisible fire is woven into the fabric of her precious gown which she alone knows about and which sustains her in her tribulations, a true treasure that cannot be taken away from her. The persisting dream of being united with one's soulmate in the outer world seems to be rooted in a pervading suspicion of an "other" within. This suggests ancestry in a bisexual primal being. Or does the myth of such ancestry come from our sense of not being whole? Whichever the case, Helga's story tells us that love of the despised as well as of that which is exalted will lead us toward the original wholeness for which we strive.

THE WORLD

The World Restored to Its Original Splendor

The woman on the World card (see image) is in step with the rhythm of the universe as she jumps out of the blue in nude splendor, framed by the laurel wreath of her glory. She is the Fool become conscious through her many tribulations on the journey to freedom. In the system of Tarot, the astrological correspondence to this last card of the Major Arcana is Saturn, ruler of death and rebirth. Again we are reminded of the rune poem and Saturn's identification with the *thurs* as "women's torment" (Page 175). As the *thurs* compelled the queen in "The Giantess on the Stoneboat" to find a resolution to her dilemma, so Saturn has been the driving force behind the success of the female depicted on this card. Her two magic wands suggest mastery over both hemispheres of the brain, the violet undulating scarf implies integration of serpent wisdom as well as the merging of the feminine red and the masculine blue into the one color of a more elevated state. She is at one with the world.

In "The Outcast," the world is reborn, not through the Word of an external celestial god, but through gestation and internal cyclic processing where trial and error finally lead to a breakthrough as is conveyed by the powerful conception / birthing metaphor of the quakes that shake the cave. This is how I see it: When Helga arrives home safely with the fire and her lover in her heart, she is the Morning Star heralding a new principle based on Love that will replace the worldview personified by her *old* father. And let us note that the transition takes place–I do not say without bloodshed–but without a killing. An admonition that forces the players to look their evil in the eye and grow up is a more productive punishment and points the way out of the vindictive mindset that poisons the world.

As the Morning Star, Venus is one with Lucifer "the lightbearer." On her quest, Helga has gone down to the underworld and redeemed Lucifer who was cast down to Hell for his arrogance. It was his arrogance that brought on him the name of Satan and Devil.

Arrogance is what characterizes the behavior of the older sisters in the tale. And their father's contemptuous words about Helga, whom he treats in an inhuman way, reveal how he prides himself above Nature. Through Helga's humble but courageous interaction with the superhuman powers, the world is restored to its original splendor. As far as we, her sisters, are concerned, we are faced with the challenge of redeeming our shadows and finding Helga in ourselves and thereby transforming the patriarchal principle by which we live into a partnership principle, be it in creation or procreation. Or have you not wondered, as I have, what is the role in this, as in so many other tales, of the "hidden" wife and mother?

Finally, we should be aware that, though Helga is the paragon of courage on her quest for the fire, there is a marked difference between her story and that of Freyja's acquisition of Brísingamen. Freyja acted not out of obedience but on her own desire. She was attracted toward the sacred union in the cave, although primitive fear may have compelled those who carried her myth forth to present it in a grotesque light. And in contrast to Freyja, who searches through foreign lands for her wild spirit-husband crying tears of red-gold, Helga waits for her soulmate to come and claim her. In that respect, it would seem that she incarnates the submissive female role of her time. But from another viewpoint, it could be said that Helga has brought the quest that Freyja initiated to a successful end. The latter's painful separation from her husband Od may have been a prerequisite for an eventual reunion on a more mature level. Helga is whole in herself.

There is nothing missing. Like attracts like. She is now prepared to enter a relationship with another as an equal.

Bibliography

Aguirre, Edwin L. "Imaging a Solar Eclipse" in *Sky & Telescope*, obt. Jan. 11, 2003 at http://www.skyandtelescope.com/article_99_1.asp.

Amberstone, Ruth Ann and Wald. *The Tarot School Correspondence Course*. www.TarotSchool.com

ARAS website: http://aras.org/

Árnason, Jón. *Íslenzkar þjóðsögur og ævintýri*, I-VI. Reykjavík, 1961.

Bettelheim, Bruno. "The Sleeping Beauty" in *The Uses of Enchantment: The Meaning and Importance of Fairy Tales* (1975). New York, 1989.

Birkhäuser-Oeri, Sibylle. Ed. Marie-Louise von Franz. *The Mother: Archetypal Image in Fairy Tales* (1977). Tr. from German by Michael Mitchell. Inner City Books, 1988.

Bjarnason, Þóroddur. "Konur": review of the exhibit *Women of the World* in *Morgunblaðið*, April 5th 2004.

Björnsson, Páll. *Kennimark kölska (Character bestiae)*. Prep. for publication by Lýður Björnsson. Reykjavík, 1976.

Biederman, Hans. *Dictionary of Symbolism: Cultural Icons and the Meanings Behind Them* (1989). Tr. from German by James Hulbert. New York, 1992.

Bolen, Jean Shinoda. *Crossing to Avalon: A Woman's Midlife Pilgrimage*. Harper, San Francisco, 1994.

Briem, Ólafur (ed.). *Eddu kvæði*, I & II. Reykjavík, 1985.

Campbell, Joseph with Bill Moyers. *The Power of Myth*. Ed. Betty Sue Flowers. New York, 1988.

Case, Paul Foster. *The Tarot: A Key to the Wisdom of the Ages*. Richmond, VA, 1947.

Charbonneau-Lassay, Louis. *The Bestiary of Christ* (1940). Tr. from French by D. M. Dooling. Arkana Books, 1992.

Eberhard, Wolfram. *A Dictionary of Chinese Symbols: Hidden Symbols in Chinese Life and Thought*. Tr. from German by G. L. Campbell. Rutledge, 1986.

Edinger, Edward F. *Anatomy of the Psyche: Alchemical Symbolism in Psychotherapy* (1985). Illinois, 1993.

Elder, George R. "Menstruating Female Figure"; "Woman Carrying a Phallus"; "The Cerne Abbas Giant" in *The Body: An Encyclopedia of Archetypal Symbolism*, vol. 2. Shambala, 1996.

Ellis Davidson, Hilda. *Roles of the Northern Goddess*. Routledge, 1998.

Eyrbyggja saga. Ed. Einar Ól. Sveinsson and Matthías Þórðarson. Reykjavík, 1935.

Frazer, Sir James G. "Chapter LX - Between Heaven and Earth" in *The Golden Bough* (1922). New York, 1958.

Gill, Elizabeth Josephine. *The Gill Tarot Deck*. U.S. Game Systems, Inc., 1990.

Grahn, Judy. *Blood, Bread, and Roses: How Menstruation Created the World*. Boston, 1993.

Holy Bible. New King James Version. United Bible Societies, 1991.

Høst, Annette. "Blessed by the Moon: Initiation into Womanhood." http://www.shamanism.dk/

Icelandic Annals 1400-1800, 1-6. Reykjavík, 1922-1988.

Íslensk orðabók. Ed. Mörður Árnason. Reykjavík, 2002.

Jahan, Ishrat in *Women of the World: A Global Collection of Art*. Pomegranate, San Francisco, 2000.

Jakobsdóttir, Svava. *Gunnlaðar saga*. Reykjavík, 1987.

Jakobsdóttir, Svava. "Gunnlöð og hinn dýri mjöður" in *Skírnir*, haust 1988.

Jónsson, Guðni (ed.). "Sörla þáttr" and "Völsunga saga" in *Fornaldar sögur Norðurlanda*, I. Reykjavík, 1976.

Jung, C. G. *Alchemical Studies*, Vol. 13 (1976). Tr. from German by R. F. C. Hull. Princeton University Press, 1983.

Jung, C. G. *The Archetypes and the Collective Unconscious*, Vol. 9, Part 1 (1959). Tr. from German by R. F. C. Hull. Princeton University Press, 1990.

Jung, C. G. *Memories, Dreams, Reflections* (1961). Rec. and Ed. by Aniela Jaffé. Tr. from German by Richard and Clara Winston. Vintage Books, 1989.

Jung, C. G. *Psychology and Alchemy*, Vol. 12 (1953). Tr. from German by R. F. C. Hull. Princeton University Press, 1993.

Jung, Emma and von Franz, Marie-Louise. *The Grail Legend* (1960). Tr. from German by Andrea Dykes. Princeton University Press, 1970.

Knight, Chris. *Blood Relations: Menstruation and the Origins of Culture*. Yale University Press, 1991.

Lewis, Charleton T. and Short, Charles. *A Latin Dictionary*. Oxford at the Clarendon Press, 1879.

Líndal, Sigurður (ed). *Saga Íslands*, I. Reykjavík, 1974.

Lindow, John. "Máni" in *Norse Mythology: A Guide to the Gods, Heroes, Rituals and Beliefs.* Oxford University Press, 2001.

MacCulloch, John Arnott (ed.). *The Mythology of All Races*, vol. II. Boston, 1930.

Magnússon, Ásgeir Blöndal. *Íslensk orðsifjabók.* Reykjavík, 1989.

Magnusson, Magnus. *Viking: Hammer of the North.* New York, 1985.

Man, Myth & Magic: An Illustrated Encyclopedia of the Supernatural, vol. 14. Ed. Richard Cavendish. New York, 1970.

Moon, Beverly, ed. "The Ecstasy of Saint Teresa" in *An Encyclopedia of Archetypal Symbolism*, vol. 1. Shambala, 1997.

Motz, Lotte. "Gerðr" in *Maal og Minne*, 1981.

Neumann, Erich. "On the Moon and Matriarchal Consciousness." Tr. from German by Hildegard Nagel. *Spring*, 1954.

Neumann, Erich. *The Great Mother: An Analysis of the Archetype* (1955). Tr. from German by Ralph Manheim. Princeton, NJ, 1991.

Njáls saga (Brennu-Njáls saga), ed. Einar Ól. Sveinsson. Reykjavík, 1954.

Nordal, Sigurður. *Völuspá.* Reykjavík, 1952.

Norris, Pamela. *Eve: A Biography.* New York University Press, 1999.

Olds, Sharon. *The Wellspring.* New York, 1996.

Pálsson, Hermann. *Völuspá.* Reykjavík, 1994.

Place, Robert M. *Alchemy and the Tarot.* New York, 2011.

Pollack, Rachel. *Tarot Wisdom: Spiritual Teachings and Deeper Meanings.* Llewellyn Publications, 2008.

The Rider-Waite Tarot Deck. U.S. Games Systems, Inc., 1971.

Ragnheidardottir, Hallfridur. "Freyja" & "Sleipnir" at http://www.dreamsandtarot.is/

Ragnheidardottir, Hallfridur. "Menstruation" in the ARAS *Book of Symbols: Reflections on Archetypal Images.* Ed.-in-chief Ami Ronnberg. Taschen, 2010.

Raven, Arlene. "As the World Turns," foreword to *Women of the World: A Global Collection of Art.* Pomegranate, San Francisco, 2000.

"Sacrifice" in *Encyclopaedia Britannica*, 1984.

Schapira, Laurie Layton. *The Cassandra Complex: Living with Disbelief.* BookSurge, www.booksurge.com, 1988.

Schneiders, Toni. Photograph of Frija in *Larousse World Mythology* (1965). Ed. Pierre Grimal. Hamlyn, 1989.

Sharp, Daryl. *Jung Lexicon*. Inner City Books, 1991.

Shuttle, Penelope and Redgrove, Peter. *The Wise Wound: The Myths, Realities, and Meanings of Menstruation*. New York, 1988.

Sigurðsson, Gísli (ed.). *Úr Mímisbrunni: Hávamál, Völuspá, Gylfaginning*. Reykjavík, 1994.

Sigurðsson, Gísli (ed.). *Eddukvæði*. Reykjavík, 1998.

Simek, Rudolf. *Hugtök og heiti í norrænni goðafræði*. Ed. Heimir Pálsson, tr. from German by Ingunn Ásdísardóttir. Reykjavík, 1993.

Sturluson, Snorri. *Edda*. Prep. for publication by Guðni Jónsson. Reykjavík, 1935.

Sturluson, Snorri. "Ynglinga saga" and "Hákonar saga góða" in *Heimskringla*, I. Ed. Bjarni Aðalbjarnarson. Reykjavík, 1979.

Sæmundsson, Matthías Viðar. *Galdrar á Íslandi: Íslensk galdrabók*. Reykjavík, 1992.

Sæmundsson, Matthías Viðar. "Upplýsingaröld 1750-1840" in *Íslensk bókmenntasaga*, 3. Reykjavík, 1996.

Taylor, Jill Bolte. *My Stroke of Insight* (2006). Plume, 2009.

Teresa of Ávila. *Interior Castle*. Tr. and ed. by E. Allison Peers. Doubleday, 2004.

Thorsteinsson, Steingrímur. *Ævintýrabók*. Reykjavík, 1947.

Von Franz, Marie-Louise. *The Interpretation of Fairy Tales* (1974), rev. ed. Shambala, 1996.

Von Franz, Marie-Louise with Fraser Boa. *The Way of the Dream*. Toronto, 1988.

Weideger, Paula. *Menstruation and Menopause: The Physiology and Psychology, the Myth and the Reality*. New York, 1976.

Pronunciation of Icelandic letters

á: [ou]	down	æ: [ī]	die
au: [œj]	Fr. feuil	ö: [ė]	word
í: [ē]	eel	ð, Ð: [TH]	though
ó: [ō]	tow	þ, Þ: [th]	thorn
ú: [oo]	foot		

Glossary[1]

Alchemy: In the words of Robert M. Place "alchemy is the ancient ancestor of modern medicine, chemistry, physics, depth psychology, and occultism." (*Alchemy and the Tarot*, 13). These disciplines, today considered separate subjects, were all one to the alchemists whose ultimate goal was to create the philosophers' stone, an elusive substance that could transmute lead into gold. Carl Jung, who discovered in the writings of the alchemists a parallel to his theory of individuation, concluded that they had projected their inner processes onto the substances they worked with in their laboratories. From the Jungian perspective the philosophers' stone is an archetypal image of wholeness toward which the individuation process evolves.

Archetypal image: The form or representation of an archetype in consciousness.

Archetype: Primordial, structural elements of the human psyche.

Aurgelmir: Another name of Ymir, the primordial giant.

Ásgarðr [Asgard]: Abode of the Æsir.

Æsir (*sing. masc.* ás, *fem.* ásynja): Collective name for the gods and goddesses presided over by Odin.

Bragi: God of poetry.

Brynhildr [Brynhild]: Valkyrie, warrior maiden. She was stung with a sleeping thorn by Odin for disobedience and awakened by Sigurd the dragon-slayer on Doe-Mountain.

Ego: Central complex in the field of consciousness. Not to be confused with the self, to which the ego is subordinate.

Freyja: Goddess of love and fertility and daughter of the Vanir-god Njord. Her attribute was the necklace Brísingamen. She taught the art of *seiðr*, an ecstatic rite of divination, to Odin and the Æsir. When Freyja journeyed, her chariot was pulled by two cats. She had a liking for love song. Her name means "Lady."

Freyr: Son of the Vanir-god Njord and the most important fertility god in Norse mythology. His name means "Lord." His attribute was a golden boar called Gullinbursti.

Frigg: Wife of Odin and mother of his son Baldur.

---

1 Definitions of **archetypal image, archetype, ego, projection, self, shadow, wholeness** are taken, with permission, from *Jung Lexicon* by Daryl Sharp. Inner City Books, 1991.

Gerðr [Gerd]: Daughter of the giant Gymir (personification of the ocean). She became the wife of Freyr with whom, according to Snorri Sturluson's *Ynglinga saga*, she had the son Fjölnir.

Ginnungagap [Gap of Ginnungar]: Primordial void.

Gunnlöð [Gunnlöd]: Guardian of the mead of poetry.

Iðunn [Idun]: Wife of Bragi, god of poetry. She kept the gold apples of eternal youth in her ashen box.

Jón Árnason (1819-1888): Icelandic writer, librarian and pioneering collector of Icelandic folk tales.

Jung, Carl Gustav (1875-1961): Swiss psychiatrist and psychotherapist, founder of analytical psychology.

Loki: A mercurial trickster-figure who embodies the dual nature of a *thurs* and a god; personification of Odin's shadow side for good or for ill (see shadow).

Máni: Personification (*masc.*) of the moon.

Nerthus: Germanic goddess who, according to the Roman historian Tacitus (55?-120? AD), was venerated as *Terra mater* ('Mother Earth') on an island in the Baltic in the first century AD. Her role was overtaken by Njord whose name is etymologically identical to that of Nerthus.

Njörðr [Njord]: A Vanir-god of fertility venerated by farmers and also by seafarers and fishermen. He was later absorbed into the pantheon of the Æsir, as were his children Freyja and Freyr. Njord was the husband of Skadi who left him for a life in the mountains.

Óðinn [Odin]: The foremost god in Norse mythology and the father of all. Odin was a god of war and master of magic, wisdom and the word. Odin's steed was the eight-legged Sleipnir, his attribute the spear Gungnir.

Óðr [Od]: Freyja's husband who went far away while she stays behind, crying tears of red gold. "Poetry" and "wildness" are embedded in his name. He fathered Freyja's daughter *Hnoss* ("Treasure").

Projection: An automatic process whereby contents of one's own unconscious are perceived to be in others.

Self: The archetype of wholeness and the regulating center of the psyche; transpersonal power that transcends the ego. Its essential nature is unknowable, as is the essential nature of any archetype, but its manifestations are the content of myth and legend. Experiences of the self possess a numinosity characteristic of religious revelations. According to Jung ("The Mana Personality" in CW7, par. 399), the self might equally be called the "God within us."

Shadow: Hidden unconscious aspects of oneself, both good and bad, which the ego has either repressed or never recognized.

Sigurðr [Sigurd]: Legendary hero and Odin's protégé. Slayer of the dragon Fáfnir.

Sigyn: Wife of Loki.

Skaði [Skadi]: Daughter of a giant and the wife of Njord, whom she later left and settled on her father's domain in the mountains where she runs on skis and hunts with bow and arrow. Skadi was called the "chaste bride of gods."

Skírnir: Freyr's lackey and hero of the Lay of Skírnir who rides to *Jötunheimar*, the world of giants, and coerces Gerd to accept the proposal of his lovesick master.

Snorri Sturluson (1179-1241): Icelandic chieftain, historian and poet. Author of the *Prose Edda* and *Heimskringla*, a history of the Norwegian kings.

Steingrímur Thorsteinsson (1831-1913): Icelandic poet and translator into Icelandic of works like Hans Christian Andersen's *Fairy Tales* and *One Thousand and One Nights*.

Vanir: Collective name of the fertility gods venerated by farmers, and also by seafarers and fishermen who depended on fair winds and good weather.

Völva: seeress, sibyl. Her attribute was a staff. Freyja was a *völva*, and so was Gunnlöd from whom Odin stole the mead of poetry.

Wholeness: A state in which consciousness and the unconscious work together in harmony. In terms of individuation, where the goal is a vital connection with the self, Carl Jung contrasted wholeness with the conflicting desire to become perfect.

Ymir: Primordial giant. The name is *masc.* and means "twin." Odin and his brothers Vili and Vé created the earth and the sky from his dismembered body.

Þór [Thor]: Son of Odin and Earth. He was a god of thunder, strongest amongst the Æsir, an unswerving protector of gods and men and sworn enemy of giants. His attribute was the hammer Mjöllnir. It is the warrior with his hammer aloft who impresses himself on us in the myths. But as fertilizing rain is the counterpart of thunder and lightening, there is another less flaunted side to Thor. Rock carvings from the Bronze Age show an ithyphallic Thor consecrating the marriage of an embracing couple with his hammer. (Simek, 280) Thor's hammer was thus a dual symbol of raw, destructive force and fertilizing power. His chariot was pulled by two he-goats.

Þurs [thurs]: Derogatory denomination for a giant; name of the Þ-rune.

Index

g

union 14, 24, 29, 38, 55, 76, 84, 108, 115, 201, 205; celestial 4; heavenly 3, 71; sexual 16
unity 25, 113, 151, 169; beyond opposites 25; restored 147
universal v, xv, xvi, 24, 41, 59, 128, 178
universe, rhythm of 204
uterus 12, 110

vagina 26, 79
Valhalla 53, 122
Valkyrie 52, 53, 58, 88, 89, 93, 94, 95, 170, 194, 211
Vanir 29, 30, 116, 121, 170, 171, 176, 211, 212, 213
Venus 51, 126, 204
vessel 13, 45, 77, 83, 90, 93, 104, 110, 129, 135, 152, 165, 200
 See also cauldron
victim xviii, 20, 31, 50, 54, 69, 75, 94, 115, 137, 146, 154, 165
virgin 11, 20, 52, 93, 130, 135; birth 121; saintly 43
vision(s) 20, 24, 27, 78, 85, 88, 118, 147, 184, 193
visionary 84, 151, 157
von Franz, Marie-Louise 41, 42, 67, 68, 120, 121, 207, 208, 210
Vón, river called 197
vulva 6, 20, 26, 137, 143, 152, 176, 182, 194; symbolic 60
Völsunga saga ("Saga of the Völsungs") 54, 94, 95, 168, 170, 208
Völuspá ("Prophecy of the Seeress") 14, 27, 71, 72, 94, 122, 129, 130, 144, 179, 197, 209, 210
Völuspá in skamma ("Short Prophecy of the Seeress") 129

völva 2, 5, 6, 16, 26, 27, 47, 52, 56, 71, 72, 73, 82, 85, 117, 118, 120, 122, 127, 129, 130, 131, 132, 133, 144, 145, 147, 152, 155, 157, 169, 179, 197, 198, 213

war 15, 16, 23, 46, 52, 53, 95, 113, 122, 133, 144, 212
weaving 6, 70, 88, 94, 95
web 94; of fate 94
Weideger, Paula 14, 45, 51, 210
wellspring 113, 154, 209; creative 24, 169
wholeness 8, 24, 71, 72, 76, 79, 87, 195, 200, 211, 212, 213; original 75, 202
whore 7, 9, 73, 81, 101, 122, 128, 193; menstrual blood of 7, 9, 75, 81
wife 7, 17, 20, 29, 45, 52, 63, 64, 69, 81, 82, 89, 92, 95, 97, 98, 107, 108, 112, 120, 123, 124, 125, 126, 127, 130, 136, 137, 146, 159, 160, 164, 167, 171, 173, 177, 178, 184, 185, 194, 205, 212, 213
will xx, 8, 44, 52, 53, 57, 84, 95, 98, 99, 115, 122, 137; free 109
wine 4, 5, 93, 99, 101, 115, 116, 130, 136, 183
wise woman vi, 2, 35, 52; 13th 23, 38, 43, 46, 49, 50, 51, 55, 56, 58, 59, 60
witch 17, 37, 77, 92, 123, 126, 127, 128, 129, 133, 134, 136, 137, 155, 182, 194, 197; -craft 124, 145; hunt 52, 54
wolf 47, 129, 130, 131, 136, 137, 197, 198
womb; weeping 14, 153
worm(s) 78, 85, 131, 132, 194
wound xi, 26, 44, 52, 59, 60, 94, 107, 137, 143, 210

Ymir 69, 72, 75, 76, 77, 78, 79, 81, 83, 85, 86, 87, 89, 121, 174, 193, 211, 212, 213
yule 134

Hallfridur J. Ragnheidardottir is a poet and a dreamworker with M.A. in Icelandic literature. In her master's thesis she explored her mythological heritage through the lens of Jungian psychology. It was the beginning of an adventurous journey in search of her own music. In this book, she gives voice to her passion for myth, dreams, tarot and poetry. From 1970 her life has been divided between New York and Reykjavik, where she and her husband have now settled. Their son, daughter-in-law and two grandsons live in New York, keeping alive the connection between the two cities.

CPSIA information can be obtained at www.ICGtesting.com
Printed in the USA
BVOW07s2030260216

438125BV00009B/4/P